Lyme Disease Update:
Science, Policy, & Law

Marcus Cohen

Editor Patricia V. Smith
Foreword by Brian Fallon, MD
Preface by Amy Tan

Lyme Disease Association, Inc. – New Jersey 2004

Lyme Disease Association, Inc.
PO Box 1438
Jackson New Jersey 08527

www.LymeDiseaseAssociation.org

This book is intended to provide practical and useful information on the subject matter covered. However, it is being distributed with the understanding that the Lyme Disease Association in not engaged in rendering medical or other professional services. If medical or other expert assistance is required, the services of a competent professional should be sought.

Library of Congress Catalog Card Number 2004108194

ISBN 0-9758776-0-7
Printed in Canada

*This book is dedicated to all
those who have suffered because of Lyme disease
and to the memory of John Drulle, MD,
a dedicated Lyme disease pioneer.*

Acknowledgments

The Lyme Disease Association's *Lyme Disease Update: Science, Policy, & Law* is written by Marcus Cohen, a columnist for the *The Townsend Letter for Doctors and Patients* and edited by Patricia Smith, President, Lyme Disease Association (LDA). The preface is written by *New York Times* best-selling author Amy Tan and the Foreword by Brian Fallon, MD, Professor of Clinical Psychiatry, Columbia University College of Physicians & Surgeons.

Compiling a work such as this is more than a one-person job. Author and LDA thank the above individuals for their contributions to this work, especially Dr. Brian Fallon, for his insights and forward, and Amy Tan for her preface.

Cover Photo

LDA acknowledges and thanks David W. Dorward, PhD, National Institutes of Health, Rocky Mountain Labs, Montana, for the cover photo of the *Borrelia burgdorferi* (and below) showing a scanning electron microscope image of the penetration of human B cells by *Borrelia burgdorferi* at a magnification of approximately 13,700.

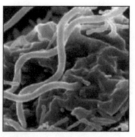

The following individuals were instrumental in providing motivation and information for, and guidance of this work: Diane Blanchard; Jeanine DerBedrosian; Jim Derbedrosian; Tom Grier; Nick Harris, PhD; Richard Horowitz, MD, Lorraine Johnson, Esq.; Ellen Lubarsky; Ed Masters, MD; Ira Mauer, Esq.; Phyllis Mervine; Polly Murray; Lynn Oliver; Steve Phillips, MD; Joni Schultz; Harold Smith, MD; Sharon Smith; Ted Sussan, Esq; Kim Uffleman; Judy Weeg; Pam Weintraub; and the Massachusetts Department of Health. We apologize if we have missed anyone else who contributed his or her time to ensure the accuracy of this reference book.

Contents

Foreword

Lyme disease first came to the attention of public health authorities in the United States when a mother in Lyme, Connecticut, reported an unusual clustering of cases of arthritis among children in her neighborhood. Although this woman's telephone calls and letters were at first ignored by the health authorities, eventually her persistence paid off, and clinical researchers focused their energies on this newly recognized disease. Lyme disease initially was thought to be a disease restricted to a rash followed by arthritis that was not infectious in origin. Within several years, however, it became clear that the disease was caused by a tick-borne spiral-shaped bacterium which, when transmitted to a human, could cause prominent dermatologic, rheumatologic, cardiac, neurologic, psychiatric, and ophthalmologic manifestations.

The early days of Lyme disease in Connecticut for the clinical scientists were ones of exciting discovery. Researchers realized that this agent, like the spirochete that causes syphilis, could lodge in the body, remain dormant, only to become active months or years later. Because the manifestations were protean and could suggest other diseases, Lyme disease was dubbed the "New Great Imitator," replacing syphilis for that distinction. Excitement in discovery was replaced by a sobering recognition that some patients relapsed after an initial course of antibiotic therapy and that the laboratory tests were problematic, plagued by both false negative and false positive results.

Lyme disease created a major problem for many patients and their families. Faced with frightening multi-systemic symptoms, uncertainty about diagnosis, and uncertainty about treatment, patients were left not knowing whom to trust within the medical community. Despite the CDC's repeated statements that Lyme disease is a diagnosis that is made based on clinical criteria, some doctors in academic settings and in the community became more and more reliant on laboratory tests, refusing to make the clinical diagnosis and treat the patient unless the lab tests came back positive. Patients who became very sick after a tick bite and flu-like illness with typical Lyme symptoms were being turned away from the very doctors they had trusted so much.

The failure of the medical profession to acknowledge and address the complexities of disseminated Lyme disease led to the emergence of patient advocacy groups. These groups, composed of patients and concerned family members, organized educational meetings and support groups, raised funds to support research, and met with local and national politicians to bring the full strength of our governmental resources to help in the fight against Lyme disease. While much has been learned about Lyme disease, there is still a great deal that puzzles clinicians and challenges scientists and public health authorities.

This valuable document – *Lyme Disease Update* – reflects the passionate commitment of the Lyme Disease Association to educate others about Lyme disease. Carefully referenced and written by Marcus Cohen in a style that is accessible to both the medical professional and the educated non-medical person, this document provides overviews and digests of important research findings from the last few decades. No update can be fully comprehensive. This *Update*, however, does do an excellent job of providing the reader with an opportunity to learn about some of the pivotal studies in Lyme disease and about areas of research that need to be more aggressively pursued.

The Lyme Disease Association is a national organization with chapters and affiliates in states throughout the country. Without the commitment of the Lyme Disease Association and its affiliates and state chapters, whose ongoing efforts to promote better education, training and funding for research on Lyme disease have met with remarkable success, many of our recent advances in the battle against this insidious disease would not have been possible. Once again, as in the early days of Lyme disease, it is the patients, families, and neighbors who keep us in the medical scientific community focused on the fact that a disease that needs to be eradicated is laying siege to our communities.

Brian A. Fallon, MD
Columbia University
College of Physicians and Surgeons
April 2004

Preface

For many years, physicians and legislators have had a difficult time discerning what is fact and fiction, sensationalism and solid evidence as it pertains to a disease caused by a tiny spirochete called *Borrelia*. This spirochete is at the center of a charged controversy in the medical community over its prevalence, the methods for detecting it, and what constitutes sound medical practice for treating patients with early to late-stage borreliosis.

As more research unfolds, only the reason for the controversy is clear: Our scientific understanding of this evasive bacteria has been incomplete and only now is evolving. We do not precisely know, for example, how *Borrelia* causes changes within the human immune system, or why some patients get predominantly arthritic symptoms, while others progress almost directly to neurological involvement. We do not have complete laboratory tests that provide direct and consistent evidence that *Borrelia* is present and active, present and inactive, present and undetectable, or completely eliminated from the body following medical treatment. We do not know with scientific certainty what length of treatment is required, particularly if there are co-infections. Thus, for the time being, this is a disease that is largely known by its multi-systemic and highly variable *symptoms*.

Patients bear the consequences of these unknowns, particularly if they are misdiagnosed, under-treated, or declared cured despite progressive disease. I know this firsthand, for I was not diagnosed in the early stages, and I went on to develop late-stage neuroborreliosis. I have had this disease since 1999.

My case is in many ways typical. Like many, I had little awareness of Lyme disease, for I did not live in what was considered the tick-infested hotbeds on the East Coast. I am a Californian—that's where I file my taxes—and I live among the hills of San Francisco with its tick-free, concrete sidewalks. For a good long while it did not seem significant that I also have a home in New York, that I weekend in the country, and my main form of exercise is hiking. In addition to trekking in the woodlands of Mendocino, Sonoma, and Santa Cruz counties in California, I have also sojourned to leafy spots in Connecticut and upstate New York. I once loved to sit in the tall grass next to the river, and lean my back against a shady oak tree.

I passed off my early symptoms—a stiff neck, insomnia, a constant headache, and a bad back followed by a frozen shoulder—as the unpleasant aftermath of too much airplane travel. I was often tired and jittery, but that, I reasoned, was the consequence of an active and exciting life. Who was I to complain? I had a wonderful life, a great husband, lovely homes, a successful career. I was rarely sick and went to the doctor only for my annual checkup. Even when I came down with the fever, aches and pains of the "flu" earlier in the summer, I had managed to beat it back without developing any of the respiratory sequelae. What a great immune system I had!

When my feet grew tingly and then numb, I mentioned to my doctor that I had had an unusual rash earlier that year. It had begun with a tiny black dot that I guessed might have been a pinprick-sized blood blister. It grew more rounded as it filled, and then I either scratched it out or it fell out on its own, leaving a tiny pit and a growing red rash, which, curiously, did not itch, but lasted a month. Because that rash seemed so unusual, as did my neuropathy, I wondered aloud whether they were related. My doctor said no.

Like many chronic Lyme disease patients, as my symptoms mounted and a scattering of tests proved positive for an array of seemingly disparate conditions, I was referred to specialist after specialist, until I eventually had consulted ten and had taken countless lab tests. Because one repeated test revealed my blood sugar inexplicably dipped from time to time into the 20s and 30s without symptoms, I underwent a 48-hour fast. An MRI revealed

15 lesions in my frontal and parietal lobes, but my doctors felt that was normal for a person my age; I was 49 at the time. A CAT scan showed an incidentaloma on my adrenal gland, and that was where I hung my hopes, on a tiny benign tumor which I could excise laparoscopically in hopes of being rid of my enervating symptoms. Instead, after beginning steroids, the bizarre symptoms worsened. Hallucinations began. I saw people walking into my room, two girls jumping rope, numbers spinning on an odometer, a fat poodle hanging from the ceiling. I also had strange episodes in which I behaved strangely but had no recollection of what I had done as reported to me by others. I apparently rang people up at midnight and talked in a wispy voice. I had flung laundry around the living room. My husband said I acted at times as if I were in a trance, eyes wide open but unresponsive to his and a friend's questions. I now had nightly nightmares and acted them out, punching at lamps or my husband, and once landing on my head in a dive toward my dream assailant.

By day, my memory was held together with friable threads, my concentration was as easy to disperse as blown dust, and when I tried to read, I often found by the second page that I had no idea what the book was about. When I wrote by hand, I reversed letters. When I spoke, I substituted words with like-sounding beginnings. I did not possess any of the skills necessary to write fiction, for I was barely able to traverse the distance of sentence to sentence, let alone keep in mind a narrative that had to span four hundred pages and keep taut multiple intricacies of plot, characters, and thematic imagery. Thus, my novel-in-progress lay abandoned between feeble attempts to resuscitate it. At times, when asked what I was writing, to my horror, I could not remember, and I would struggle over the next hour trying to recall the faintest details. I no longer dared get behind the wheel of a car, because I could not process fast enough when to depress the accelerator and when the brake. When I did venture out on foot, I would sometimes find myself lost in what I knew was a familiar place, my neighborhood of thirty years. Why didn't that building on the comer look familiar? Why did everything seem as though it were the first time I had been there? I easily became lost in stores, hospitals, hotels, and I would panic, certain I was losing my mind and developing dementia related to early Alzheimer's. My anxiety was a hundredfold of what was warranted, even in a post 9/11 era. Eventually, I could no longer leave my house alone. In any case, it hurt to walk too far. My muscles were stiff, my knees and hips ached. And I was almost too tired to care anymore.

Let me add here that my doctors were affiliated with major urban hospitals, were tops in their department, well-known, well respected. I liked them. I still do. Not once did they raise the idea that I was a hypochondriac. But they also did not raise the possibility of Lyme disease. Actually, one doctor had considered the possibility that I was infected with a spirochetal bacteria, and he gave me an ELISA test, which was negative–not for Lyme–but for syphilis.

I turned to the internet, which is where doctors believe patients catch terminal illnesses, that is, whatever disease they see described before them on the terminal. And there I saw that an ELISA was also used to screen for Lyme disease. Further reading led me to see that all my symptoms could easily fall under the multi-systemic umbrella of borreliosis. Further sleuthing gave me the name of a Lyme specialist, someone my other physicians acknowledged was "a good doctor."

My Lyme specialist considered the history of my rash, the summertime flu, the migrating aches and neuropathy, the insomnia and fatigue. He thought 15 lesions in my brain were significant in light of my neurological symptoms. He saw on previous tests that I had some interesting changes in my immune system. He ordered a complete battery of tests from IGeneX, a lab specializing in tick-borne illnesses, to check for not only Lyme disease, but its common co-infections. Two weeks later, I learned I was positive for Lyme on the Western blot. My doctor told me that the test only confirmed what he already knew.

Let me hasten to add that not all chronic Lyme patients test positive on the Western blot, at least not at the levels set by doctors who follow CDC surveillance criteria as diagnostic. As this booklet outlines, there is much more to be done before the tests can be considered reliable in every lab across the country. I know this firsthand because after I started antibiotic treatment I took part in a study in which my blood was sent out to five different labs for the ELISA and Western blot. The results were all over the place—with Lyme-specific bands lighting up in one lab and not the other. There was almost not a single consistency. In addition, I had a negative ELISA test but a positive PCR, that is, I had DNA evidence of *borrelia* in my blood. And this was nine months *after* I had started antibiotic treatment.

Like many late-stage neurological Lyme patients, it took a while for symptoms to begin to lift. A day after starting antibiotic treatment, I became feverish and ill with the classic Jarisch-Herxheimer reaction. A month later, the joint and muscle pain eased up somewhat. Two months, and some of the fog finally lifted, and I frantically wrote for long days, fearful that the curtain would come down again. After six months, I had no muscle stiffness or joint pain remaining. Today, I can once again write fiction, speak at conferences, and walk in my neighborhood alone and without anxiety and panic. I've been under treatment now for over a year. I consider myself 85% improved from where I was a year ago. I still have what I call memory black holes when I am tired, and I have neuropathy in my feet, which at times becomes too painful for me to walk more than a block. I know that my late diagnosis means I am in this for years, perhaps even for life. But at least I have my mind back.

I have chosen to cite my case so you will understand why I am so excited that this book is now available to those interested in improving the standard of care to patients with this devastating and potentially progressive and fatal disease. Until now, physicians, HMOs, policymakers, and insurance companies have had to rely on partial information in giving their recommendations. This limited knowledge has been used to maintain a standard of care in serious need of updating and substantial revision. Those physicians who went beyond this old standard were sometimes treated punitively by their peers. No wonder many doctors have been reluctant to treat patients who claim to have Lyme symptoms. And for those physicians who did want to learn more about Lyme disease, there was no convenient way for them to obtain up-to-date information without gleaning through thousands of studies, some highly pertinent, others only tangentially so.

But now that has changed. Herein lies the information that is as up-to-the-moment as can be, and it clearly spells out the new course for how we must view the wily spirochete *Borrelia*. This summation provides what medical organizations and policymakers especially needed: access to *peer-reviewed* studies on *Borrelia*, borreliosis, and its associated co-infections, so that they might fully understand the problems both of relying solely on lab tests for diagnosis and using arbitrary lengths for treatment. Herein are the peer-reviewed studies on persistence of Lyme–many studies and not just one–evidence of the bacteria dividing and proliferating in late-stage cases. And at last, there is illumination on those treatment failures that have been given the elliptical and all-inclusive, or rather, inconclusive term *post-Lyme syndrome.*

The failures are not simply medical. As a patient, I have joined a club of people with a stigmatized disease that many doctors do not want to treat. While I have been lucky enough to find a doctor who is willing to provide open-ended treatment—and I have the means to pay for it—many of my fellow Lyme patients have gone without appropriate care. As a consequence, they have lost their health, their jobs, their homes, their marriages, and even their lives.

As a writer of both novels and non-fiction, I know the power of the written word on a page. It can turn hearts, open eyes, and change lives. A story is a means to see the world from a new and higher perch. And this book does exactly that. It is the story of Lyme disease. It raises the level of understanding of what it is and how pervasive it is in the United States, how pervasive it can be in the soft tissues and fluids of the body. I also found it to be compulsively readable, a page-turner.

It is my hope that physicians will make this the next book they take along for beach reading—being careful, of course, to avoid the long grassy stalks along the way to the sand. It will take just a few hours of time to finish it and that can mean a huge difference in the lifetime of patients like me.

My thanks to you for making this part of your required reading.

Amy Tan

Introduction

The idea for the *Lyme Disease Update* came to Pat Smith, President of the Lyme Disease Association (LDA), as she traveled to meetings around the US. Invariably, patients, physicians, and government officials asked her for reliable information about Lyme and its associated tick-borne diseases. They especially sought the latest scientific data in peer-reviewed journals and updates on government action. The LDA possesses a huge amount of literature on these topics, but it had nothing to offer in a single comprehensive, concise, format.

Never one to drop a useful idea, she decided to make up for this lack in the Fall of 2002. Here it is the Spring of 2004, and her idea has finally materialized. Just before the *Lyme Disease Update* went to press, Ms. Smith jotted down the following thoughts:

"Publication of the *Update* coincides with an announcement by the Centers for Disease Control and Prevention (CDC) of a 40% increase in Lyme cases nationwide. The CDC received almost 24,000 reports in 2002, a figure the CDC itself says represents only 10% of actual cases. Thus, 240,000 Americans may have contracted new cases of Lyme in 2002 alone. According to scientific evidence, 10 to 15 percent of these patients may develop persistent or recurrent disease that could affect them for years.

This book presents a significant portion of the clinical and laboratory studies revealing the secrets of the microorganism primarily responsible for Lyme in the US. It is a member of the spirochete family–slender, spirally undulating bacteria–named *Borrelia burgdorferi* (*Bb*) after Dr. Willy Burgdorfer, who discovered it at the Rocky Mountain Labs, National Institutes of Health (NIH), in the early 1980s.

A quarter of a century after identification of the cause, however, the picture surrounding Lyme disease remains cloudy. Researchers are still trying to pin down how *Bb* eludes detection by the immune system, precisely how it invades and damages major organ systems, how it can stay latent for months or recur, how it apparently escapes destruction by antibiotics.

These uncertainties continue to hinder the diagnosis and treatment of patients here and abroad. The problems in diagnosis are especially germane to the spread of this disease. The main serology tests for antibodies to *Bb*, the ELISA and Western blot, are too unreliable. Antibodies, which normally react on ELISAs, can be bound in immune complexes and not show. So patients can test negative, yet have Lyme disease. The relatively recent emergence of co-infections, contracted by the bite of the same ticks that transmit Lyme, now complicates both diagnosis and treatment.

Patients have responded to the unresolved scientific questions by forming groups to pursue answers through education and research funding. Where political advocacy has fallen short, patients and their families have turned to the judicial system, seeking redress for injury, disability, loss of income, education, and treatment expenses resulting from Lyme disease. The *Update* follows this path in its sections on Science, Policy and Law, detailing these efforts."

SCIENCE

All papers chosen for the science sections of the *Lyme Disease Update* have appeared in journals respected for publication of evidence-based, peer-reviewed findings. Because the LDA is greatly concerned about chronic or recurrent illness, which manifests in 10 to 15 percent of US patients, the *Update* presents studies on persistent infection and long-term treatment. The dates of publication range from the late 1980s to articles published during the month we were preparing to go to press.

In the "Foreword" to the *Update*, Dr. Brian Fallon recalls that "the early days of Lyme disease in Connecticut for the clinical scientists were ones of exciting discovery." But soon, he notes, "excitement in discovery was replace by a sobering recognition that some patients relapsed after an initial course of antibiotic therapy and that the laboratory tests were problematic, plagued by both false negative and false positive results."

A sense of that initial excitement pulses in reports synopsized in the *Update*. Take, for example, the three investigations by research teams led by Dr. Steven Schutzer, published in *The Lancet* (1990), the *Journal of Clinical Investigation* (1994), and *the Journal of the American Medical Association* (1999).

The first study sought an explanation for negative results in antibody tests in patients with apparent Lyme disease but no observable EM rash, focusing on the possibility of sequestration of antibody to *Bb* in immune complexes (ICs). The second looked into whether antibody specific to one of the outer surface proteins of *Bb* might form early in Lyme, yet not show because it was bound in ICs (or at levels too low to detect). The last demonstrated that formation of specific *Bb* ICs is common in active Lyme infection, detectable by existing simple methods of analysis.

As Schutzer's research advances, it leaves an impression of heightened intensity, with the scientist resembling a sleuth zeroing in on an elusive suspect.

Lyme disease, can cause suffering beyond metaphor, Lyme takes relatively few lives, but it can miserably diminishing the quality of life for patients unable to recover from infection. In addition to the real risk of adverse reaction to protracted antibiotics, lengthy courses of antibiotics can be expensive.

In its *Morbidity and Mortality Weekly Report*, 6/4/99, the CDC estimated the cost of treating various complications of Lyme as opposed to the cost of prompt, effective treatment: $6,845 for cardiac sequelae; $34,304 for chronic arthritis; $61,193 for neurologic sequelae; early Lyme without complications, $161.

Acutely aware of the huge dollar differences, insurers often deny reimbursement for long-term treatment of persistent Lyme by labeling both "unproven." Key questions do remain unsettled in

Lyme disease, and more research is necessary to develop findings on these questions, matching new data with hypotheses to determine if the latest facts support the theories.

At this juncture in the history of Lyme disease, a number of specialists believe Lyme is overdiagnosed, that something other than active infection causes late manifestations in many cases. A number of specialists believe infection can persist or recur, and feel that Lyme is underdiagnosed. Reflecting this divergence of opinion, two standards of care have emerged in the clinical community.

Now, following the recent publication of evidenced-based guidelines for the management of Lyme disease in the scientific literature by the International Lyme and Associated Diseases Society (ILADS), a professional medical society, two sets of recommendations on diagnosis and treatment exist, with the ILADS guidelines addressing all patients with Lyme, including those with persistent, recurrent, and refractory disease.[1] This situation is neither unprecedented nor uncommon in clinical practice, where "there is seldom a single correct answer to a medical problem."[2]

Meanwhile, as part of the process of peer review, which customarily has played the lead role in answering questions about disease, Dr David Cassarino and a team including Dr. Paul Duray, Laboratory of Pathology, National Cancer Institute, NIH, in a case report published in 2004, confirmed the first evidence of striatonigral degeneration in a patient with well documented *Bb* infection of the CNS and clinical Lyme-associated parkinsonism. The patient had presented with an EM, joint pains and tremors; serum and CSF tests for antibodies and PCR for Bb were positive. Clinical parkinsonism was diagnosed by several neurologists.

---

[1] International Lyme & Associated Diseases Society, Evidence-based guidelines for the management of Lyme disease, *Expert Rev. Anti-infect. Ther.*2(1), Suppl.(2004)

[2] Wennberg JE, Outcomes research, cost containment and the fear of health-care rationing, *The New England Journal of Medicine*, 10/25/90.

Despite being treated with multiple courses of antibiotics, the patient died five years after infection. [3]

Dr. Brian Fallon, at the College of Physicians and Surgeons, Columbia University, is in the fourth and last year of an NIH-funded study of long-term treatment in neuropsychiaric Lyme. (The LDA had given Fallon a "seed" grant for a preliminary study that produced the results he used in his application to NIH.)

Dr. Mario Philippe, at Tulane University, having reported on isolating live spirochetes from chronically arthritic joints, is about to report on similar attempts to isolate live *Bb* spirochetes from the brains of rhesus monkeys.

The results of these ongoing investigations, says Dr. Fallon in an unpublished memorandum, "be they positive or negative, will supply additional evidence about the pathophysiology of persistent Lyme symptoms and the usefulness of long-term antibiotics in such cases."

Tick vectors that carry Lyme transmit microorganisms responsible for other diseases in humans; chiefly babesiosis, ehrlichioses, bartonella, and Rocky Mountain spotted fever. Many physicians have a limited knowledge of these associated conditions, which can be asymptomatic. How many Americans are infected by each disease, how many go undiagnosed and therefore untreated, and how many become infected concurrently with Lyme are questions not easily answered at present. Patients with Lyme and undiagnosed co-infections, however, may be unresponsive to Lyme therapy alone. The last science section of the *Update* offers essential information about these associated tick-borne diseases.

A "Glossary" at the end of the *Lyme Disease Update* explains technical research and medical terms appearing in the science sections.

---

[3] Cassarino, D et al, Lyme-Associated Parkinsonism: A neuropathologic case study and review of the literature, *Archives of Pathology and Laboratory Medicine*:Vol.127, No.9, pp1204-06

POLICY

The Policy section of the *Update* centers on political and public health issues. It largely involves the substantial population of patients and families across the US severely affected by persistent or relapsing Lyme.

These are the people who tend to raise the first alerts about Lyme disease to officials and representatives at the local, county, state, and federal levels of government. These are the people whose educational efforts continue to help initiate legislation and regulations aimed at managing or preventing Lyme and its associated tick-borne diseases. They have also been a source of grants to advance research on Lyme disease.

Bearing witness as a Lyme patient, novelist Amy Tan captures the plight of patients with chronic infection in her "Preface" to the *Update*:

> "While I have been lucky enough to find a doctor who is willing to provide open-ended treatment–and I have the means to pay for it–many of my fellow Lyme patients have gone without appropriate care. As a consequence, they have lost their health, their jobs, their homes, their marriages, and even their lives."

Despite fatigue and pain due to illness, these patients have succeeded in moving legislative and executive branches of government–and at least one national organization–to come to grips with the effects of Lyme disease on Americans.

In August 2002, the New England Governors' Conference passed a resolution encouraging, among other cooperative activities, state and regional surveillance of Lyme cases, state and regional initiatives to prevent or reduce the incidence of Lyme and its co-infections, and increased federal funding of studies to improve diagnosis and treatment. Patients and Lyme advocacy groups supplied the impetus for this joint statement.

In 1999, CDC in association with FDA, NIH, and the Department of Defense held a workshop to discuss tick-borne diseases and the blood supply. The Red Cross was a major participant at the event. According to a Red Cross memo, the participants concluded that there appeared to be little evidence for transmission of Ehrlichia, Rocky Mountain spotted fever, or Lyme (there was clear evidence that babesia was transmissible through blood); however, they also anticipated that the FDA would use the information presented there as a basis for developing future policies regarding tick-borne diseases.

A year or so later, the national Red Cross revised its blood donor guidelines. Previously, the guidelines permitted people to donate following treatment for Lyme. The new guidelines bar patients diagnosed with chronic Lyme. Former Lyme patients can still give blood if they have taken antibiotics and completely recovered–they can give blood 12 months after last dose of antibiotics. The American Society of Clinical Pathologists (ASCP) in its guidelines recommends deferring blood donations from all Lyme patients indefinitely. The changes suggest that the Red Cross and ASCP may have heeded the concerns of groups about the potential for transmitting *Bb* infection through blood donations.

In 2001, Lyme activists initiated a General Accounting Office (GAO) report, GAO-01-787R, to Congress on federal funding for Lyme research and on Lyme disease activities. The GAO "found that CDC, NIH, and FDA have generally met the requirements for disclosure and review of financial interests related to Lyme disease."

The GAO did note, however, that CDC was not able to provide them with some of the forms they expected to receive, and some they did receive, contained irregularities.

Senators Christopher Dodd (CT), Rick Santorum (PA) and Congressmen Virgil Goode, Jr. (MD), Joseph Pitts (PA), and Christopher Smith (NJ) requested the GAO investigation.

Over the past half-dozen years, the LDA has had meetings with various branches of the military. The first meeting took place at Aberdeen Proving Grounds, home of US Army Center for Health Promotion & Preventive Medicine (CHPPM). CHPPM displayed a prototype of new lab technology which could confirm by PCR, on the spot in the field, whether ticks that had bitten soldiers carried

Bb, so soldiers who were bitten by infected ticks could receive immediate treatment.

CHPPM also shared plans with the LDA to use GPS satellites to beam data on tick habitats–data which they have gathered since the '80s on all the major military installations in the US–and rates of infection of ticks which they were now gathering, to a special helmet worn by a soldier in the field, so that the armies could maneuver around heavy tick concentrations.

The LDA's interest in the technology the military has designed for Lyme lies in its potential for non-military use, and spurring civilian application now ranks as an LDA priority.

At a meeting arranged by Congressman Christopher Smith, NJ, in September, 2002, with top military officers from the main branches of the armed forces in Washington, DC, the LDA made presentations on persistent Lyme, stressing the difficulty in diagnosing and treating this disease. LDA also brought in a military spouse who was having difficulty receiving treatment for her Lyme disease. The military indicated that the armed forces were experiencing similar diagnostic and treatment problems in their ranks.

LAW

In our system of government, courts of law and administrative hearings serve to adjudicate contested matters not readily resolvable through the legislative and executive branches. Lyme patients have prevailed in various kinds of cases and courts. Examples of such cases, offered with explanations of the rules under which separate judicial venues operate, constitute the third part of the *Lyme Disease Update*.

When the NY Legislature relocated the Office of Professional Medical Conduct in state health department in 1975, it attached pivotal weight to the argument by doctors that they would receive a fairer hearing from colleagues than they could in the courts. Judges and juries, they felt, lacked the sophisticated training and experience that doctors had, and therefore were likely to miss the finer points in handling complaints of professional negligence, incompetence, etc.

Experts testify in court and administrative proceedings about the appropriateness or necessity of health care, and judges and juries, considering the opinions of these experts together with other kinds of testimony, have proven astute and independent in arriving at findings of fact in medical cases.

Occasionally, in such case, a judge will issue a written decision, reformulating expert views, which hits closer to home, and makes for a livelier read, than the technical language of the experts on which it is based. Witness the following pictures of the life cycle of Lyme ticks and areas likely to be endemic for them, incorporated into a ruling on a worker's compensation case from NJ in 1996. The case was decided in favor of the worker, a former golf course grounds keeper, 62-years old at the time of settlement, who claimed to be totally disabled by Lyme disease contracted during employment.

"Throughout its life cycle, the tick depends on mammalian hosts for meals. The most common hosts are mice and deer, although a variety of other animals can serve as hosts as well. Therefore, areas where there are a lot of deer (you will not see the mice), are probably at risk; the sight of deer munching on your azaleas was once heartwarming, but no longer. However, we now know that Lyme Disease occurs in areas without deer; other medium or large size animals substitute as the primary host for animal ticks. If your lawn is separated from the forest by only a little brush, then the border between the forest and your property is a prime area for ticks, suspended on grass and shrubs, as noted above. (Modern developers have taken great pride in providing a natural environment and saving as much of the forest as possible. By scalloping plots out of the forest, they have maximized the very border niche preferred by ticks and mice, and thereby have deposited new home owners in an optimal environment for Lyme Disease.)

"If you want to walk in the woods, the most likely area for tick residents would be the areas immediately adjoining deer paths.

The deer shed ticks as they walk these paths, the eggs are laid, and the ticks live in this area; ticks do not wander very far and may never see more than a few yards of the world unless carried elsewhere by a bird, dog, deer, or human. Considering the above, it is obvious that a neat lawn in suburbia, not near a forest, is not a major risk area unless it is an area frequented by deer. In general, however, lawns are a hostile environment for ticks as the ticks are more likely to dry out without shade and ground leaf clutter to protect them. A lawn in an urban area is also not an area of concern. It is the more rural areas which are at the most risk, and one can easily learn which areas are the hot spots of LD." [4]

Rural NJ was probably the setting the judge envisioned in depicting the Lyme tick's native habitat, but ticks that transmit Lyme disease and its co-infections are fast spreading into suburban America.

The *Lyme Disease Update* was conceived with the following hope, that the evidence gathered here, casting a reliable light on pieces of the Lyme puzzle still out of place, might help patients and physicians combat an infection that has escalated–in a single human generation–into the most prevalent vector-borne disease in the US; of the total number of vector-borne diseases now reported to the CDC, 95% are new Lyme cases.

Marcus A. Cohen
Manhattan, NYC
7 May 2004

---

[4] *Bird v Somerset Hills Country Club* C.P. # 94-034577.

LYME BORRELIOSIS (LYME DISEASE): An Overview

This overview gives basic information about Lyme disease. It is the sort of information one can readily find in major reference sources on current medical diagnosis and treatment for any in the wide spectrum of pathological conditions physicians may encounter in clinical practice.

Generally, the information carried in these references dwells on the common manifestations and standard therapeutic regimens for particular diseases. For many cases of suspected Lyme disease, such information may prove useful for physicians in diagnosing this infection promptly, then treating it effectively to avoid acute illness or long-term sequelae.

The percentage of Lyme patients presenting with atypical, equivocal, or non-specific signs and symptoms is uncertain. Estimates vary, but the percentage appears large enough to raise questions about the reported incidence of this illness in the US. (See "Incidence," below.)

Detailed information about diagnostic dilemmas, neurological and psychological involvement, atypical forms of the micro-organism that cause Lyme infection, long-term antibiotic therapy, and associated tick-borne diseases appears in five separate sections which follow this overview. Persistent Lyme borreliosis and appropriate therapeutic and preventive regimens for persisting illness are the major concerns of these five sections.

Cause and Transmission

The pathogen that causes Lyme disease is a spirochete, a spiral-shaped bacterium belonging to the genus *Borrelia*. Three different spirochetes make up this genus. One is responsible for septicemia in chickens. A second causes relapsing fever in humans. The third, identified in 1982 and named *Borrelia burgdorferi* (*Bb*), is the cause of Lyme infection in humans[1, 2] Scientists studying the etiologic agent for Lyme have since identified three genomic groups: *B. burgdorferi sensu stricto*, the main cause of Lyme borreliosis in the US; and *B. afzelii* and *B. garinii*, the predominant etiologic agents in Asia and Europe.[3]

Female ticks belonging to the *Ixodes ricinus* complex primarily transmit the *Bb* spirochetes to humans. These ticks bear different Latin names in various geographic regions: *Ixodes scapularis* (previously known as *I. dammini*) in the northeastern, north central, and mid-Atlantic US; *Ixodes pacificus* on the US west coast; *Ixodes ricinus* in Europe; and *Ixodes persulcatus* throughout Asia.[3, 4]

Another species of tick, *Amblyomma americanum*, the lone star tick in common usage, is believed to transmit a spirochetal illness closely resembling Lyme in the southwestern and midwestern US. The CDC calls the agent of this disease *Borrelia*

NOTE: The footnotes in the Overview for the Lyme Disease Update mostly refer to specific data and information in studies published in peer-reviewed journals. Other information here, not footnoted, can be found in such standard reference sources as Current Medical Diagnosis & Treatment (McGraw-Hill, NY).

[1] *Merriam-Webster's Medical Dictionary* (Merriam-Webster, Inc., Springfield, MA, 1995)

[2] Burgdorfer W et al, Lyme disease–a tick-borne spirochetosis? *Science* 1982; 216:1317-1319

[3] Jacobs RA, Infectious diseases: spirochetal, *Current Medical Diagnosis and Treatment* (Lange Medical Books/McGraw-Hill, NY, 39th edition, 2000).

[4] Piesman J et al, Duration of tick attachment and *Borrelia burgdorferi* transmission, *J Clin Microbiol* 1987;25:557-558.

lonestari and the disease itself, STARI, southern tick-associated rash illness. Some academic clinical researchers refer to it as "Masters' Disease," after a Missouri physician who has published extensively about it (see the Policy section of this Update, under "CDC"). In many regions of the US, *Ixodes* and *Amblyomma* ticks coexist.[5]

Ixodes ticks, commonly called deer ticks, pass through four stages of life: egg, larva, nymph, and adult. At each stage after the first, they feed once; the larvae in late summer, nymphs the following spring and summer, adults during the fall. In comparison with *Dermacentor variabilis*, the common dog tick, *Ixodes* ticks are smaller, with black legs; the nymph stages are smaller than a poppyseed. In most of the US, the white-footed mouse is the preferred host of larvae and nymphs, while adult *Ixodes* ticks prefer the white-tailed deer. In the West, woodrats and fence lizards also serve as hosts for *Ixodes pacificus* nymphs, and birds and mammals other than deer also can serve as hosts for *Ixodes pacificus* adults.

Ticks may spend several days at a blood meal. The time it takes to transmit Lyme disease to humans normally ranges from 12 to 72 hours after attachment by the tick, but there are documented cases where transmission appears to have taken less than half a day.[4, 6]

Lyme borreliosis may also be transmitted to a fetus from a pregnant woman. This occurs occasionally in certain spirochetal diseases.[7] Through PCR, polymerase chain reaction, researchers have recently discovered *Bb* DNA in human breast milk.[8]

---

[5] Barbour AG, New *Borrelia* Species. Abstract presented at the NIH, Centers for Disease, Galveston, TX, May 8-9, 1995.

[6] Patma MA et al, Disseminated Lyme disease after short-duration tick bite, *J Spirochetal and Tick-Borne Diseases* 1994; Vol. 1, No. 3:77-78.

[7] MacDonald AB, Gestational Lyme borreliosis: implications for the fetus, *Rheum Dis Clin North Am* 1989; 15(4):657-677.

[8] Schmidt BL et al, Detection of *Borrelia burgdorferi* DNA by polymerase chain reaction in the urine and breast milk of patients with Lyme borreliosis, *Diagn Microbiol Infect Dis.* 1995 Mar;21(3):121-8

Researchers have determined in animal studies that Lyme disease bacteria is transmissible through breast milk of certain animals. [8a]

Stages

Like other spirochetal infections, syphilis, for instance, Lyme borreliosis may affect several organ systems, proceed through several stages, or persist if not properly diagnosed and treated early and appropriately.

During the first stage, many patients develop erythema migrans (EM), a slightly raised or flat reddish lesion, often circular with distinct margins, at the site of the tick bite. Normally, the EM lesion expands, clears at the center, then resolves in three or four weeks. Additional frequently experienced manifestations include chills, a flu-like illness with fever, mild fatigue, and myalgia.

In a significant percentage of cases, however, no EM rash presents at all, or it develops on a part of the body patients are unlikely to notice, or the rash appears in an uncharacteristic form. Estimates of how frequently erythema migrans does not manifest, passes unnoticed, or goes unrecognized, range between 20 to 50%.[3, 9]

Passage of the *Bb* spirochete through the blood or lymph initiates the disseminated stage of Lyme borreliosis. Signs and symptoms of disseminated disease vary greatly and may occur less than a month after infection or up to a year or more afterward. Some researchers have reported that hematogenous dissemination–into the brain, for instance–may begin during the first stage, just hours after a tick bite.[10]

[8a] Altaie SS et al, Transmission of *borrelia burgdorferi* from experimentally infected mating pairs to offsprings in a murine model, SUNY at Buffalo, FDA Science Forum Abstract # I-17.

[9] Donta ST, Tetracycline therapy for chronic Lyme disease, *Clin Infect Dis* 1997; 25 Suppl 1:S52-S56.

[10] Steere, Allen, Mandell, Douglas and Bennett's Principles and Practices of Infectious Diseases 4th ed. 1995.

Reference sources on Lyme borreliosis speak of early disseminated disease (manifesting weeks or months after initial infection), and late persistent disease (manifesting many months or years after infection). In both periods, according to these sources, the illness primarily appears to involve the central nervous system, the skin, and the musculoskeletal system.

Common manifestations during the early disseminated period include secondary skin lesions, migratory pains in joints, muscle and tendon pain, a feeling of malaise, and fatigue. About 50% of patients develop the secondary skin lesions, which are not directly associated with tick bites. In this period, except for the fatigue, most of these frequent manifestations are intermittent or short in duration.

Not promptly diagnosed and treated, up to 20% of patients in the second, persistent period develop neurological disease, which can be acute. Bell's Palsy, occurring in 10% of patients with neurologic Lyme, is the most readily recognized neurologic manifestation. Encephalitis, with forgetfulness and personality changes, and aseptic meningitis, with headache and stiff neck, are other common neurological signs. These encephalitic and meningeal manifestations, accompanied by radicular pain, are collectively named "Bannwarth's Syndrome." Radiculitis, peripheral neuropathy, myelitis, chorea, and cerebellar ataxia may occur too. There can be ophthalmic involvement as well, particularly conjunctivitis, keratitis, and blindness.

Between 5 to 10% of patients with Lyme borreliosis experience cardiac involvement, usually myopericarditis leading to arrhythmias and atrioventricular heart block. Like the neurological manifestations, the heart problems during the early disseminated period can also be acute.[3]

Lyme borreliosis in the persistent period again primarily presents with neurologic or musculoskeletal involvement. More than half the patients complain of chronic arthritis, mainly of the large joints; or joint or periarticular pain, for which there are no objective findings; or synovitis, which can be permanently disabling.

The most common central and peripheral nervous system manifestations in the persistent period are encephalopathy and axonal polyneuropathy. In subacute form, the encephalopathy is characterized by problems with cognition, alterations in mood, or sleep disturbances. Radicular pain and distal sensory paresthesia are the chief signs of axonal polyneuropathy, the latter occurring in association with encephalopathy or by itself.

History

European physicians recognized a condition closely resembling Lyme borreliosis well before American physicians did, connecting the "classic" rash, erythema chronicum migrans (ECM; or, as it is now called, EM) to a tick-borne illness in 1909[11], describing a disseminated form of the illness in 1922[12], and describing a similar neurologic syndrome in 1941[13].

The first report of an *Ixodes* tick-induced rash in the US came from Wisconsin in 1970.[14] Five years later, clinical researchers associated with Yale University investigated an extraordinarily high concentration of what seemed like rheumatoid arthritis in children and adults in Lyme, CT, and several nearby towns. Believing they had come upon a new illness, they labeled it "Lyme Arthritis" and drew considerable attention through publication of their findings.[15]

Soon, though, the illness was renamed "Lyme disease" after doctors learned that it had systemic manifestations that included

---

[11] Afzelius A, Erythema chronicum migrans, *Acta Derm Venereol* (Stockh) 1921;2:120-125.

[12] Garin CH et al, Paralysie par les tiques, *J Med Lyon* 1922;3:765-767.

[13] Bannwarth A, Chronische lymphocytare meningitis, entzundliche polyneuritis und "rheumtisums," *Arch Psychiatr Nervenkr* 1941; 113:284-376.

[14] Scrimenti RJ, Erythema chronicum migrans, *Arch Dermatol* 1970;102:104-105.

[15] Steere AC et al, Lyme arthritis: an epidemic of oligoarticular arthritis of children and adults in three Connecticut communities, *Arthritis Rheum* 1977;20:7-17.

neurological, musculoskeletal, dermatologic, and cardiac components. A few years later, studies of European neuroborreliosis showed that an agent nearly identical to *Borrelia burgdorferi* causes this form of the disease, and the general name of the illness changed again–to Lyme borreliosis.

Incidence

As of this writing, Lyme borreliosis is the most prevalent vector-borne disease in the US.[16] Within the past five years, all states save Montana–now investigating reports of Lyme or Lyme-like illness–have reported cases to the Centers for Disease Control and Prevention (CDC), and the incidence is rising steeply. Over 12,000 cases were reported nationwide in 1997, nearly 17,000 in 1998, almost 24,000 cases in 2002.[17] According to the CDC, only 10% of cases are reported[17a], thus almost 240,000 actual new cases probably occurred in 2002.

Northeastern, mid-Atlantic, and north-central states have reported the great majority of new cases. An increasing number of reports from California, Florida, and Texas indicate that Lyme borreliosis has established a firm foothold in these states.

The true incidence of Lyme in the US is unknown. One limiting factor is the CDC case definition, developed for surveillance, not for clinical diagnosis and treatment. The CDC requires, for instance, a physician-diagnosed EM rash, or a positive antibody test together with major system involvement. The CDC guidelines for interpreting the Western blot (one of the main lab tests for confirming Lyme), require five of ten specific bands for IgG and two of three bands for IgM; however, there are patients with active infection whose immunoblot tests do not evidence the requisite bands.

---

[16] CDC http://www.cdc.gov/ncidod/dvbid/Lyme/qa/htm

[17] CDC MMWR 52 (31):741-750

[17a] Meade, Paul, CDC The Front Line Against Lyme disease, *Herald News* May 4, 2004, NJ.

A number of factors may account for the growing incidence of Lyme borreliosis, chief among them: suburban sprawl into rural areas around the country; the decline of open farmlands, and the corresponding resurgence of wooded areas around homes even in suburban developments; the proliferation of the white-tailed deer in closer proximity to humans; and the spread of tick vectors to new geographic regions.

The US Department of Health and Human Services (Office of Desease Prevention and Health Promotion) initiative, Healthy People 2010, challenges everyone to take steps to ensure good health. One of its 467 specific objectives is to reduce Lyme disease from a baseline 17.4 new cases / 100,000 in 92-96 to 9.7 new cases / 100,000 in endemic states.

Diagnosis

The CDC recommends that physicians suspecting Lyme borreliosis make a clinical diagnosis. Such a diagnosis may be done on two bases: (1) identification by a physician of EM in the early stage, or a major system involvement with positive serology; (2) recognition by evaluating physicians of characteristic clinical signs, a history of exposure in an area endemic for Lyme-transmitting ticks, and the use of laboratory tests as an adjunct to diagnosis.

Complicating diagnosis, some signs and symptoms can develop in one stage, others develop sequentially through all stages, and the stages can overlap. As noted earlier here, adding to the diagnostic uncertainties during the early stage, in 20 to 50 % of cases, the typical EM rash never presents, passes unnoticed, shows an atypical form, or goes unrecognized. Moreover, up to a third of Lyme patients do not recall a tick bite.[18]

For confirmation, direct detection of the *B. burgdorferi* spirochete through present methods of laboratory cultivation or visualization remains difficult; the spirochetes appear to be sparse

---

[18] Fallon BA et al, Lyme disease: a neuropsychiatric illness, *Am J Psychiatry* 1994;151:1571-1583.

in number, and they are generally found in tissue instead of blood.[19]

The lab tests overwhelmingly ordered by clinicians and researchers to support a diagnosis of Lyme borreliosis, the ELISA and Western blot (also called "immunoblot"), supply indirect evidence for the presence of *Bb*; both measure the immune system's response to the Lyme spirochete rather than looking for the components of the spirochete itself.

In a Lyme ELISA, the methodology basically involves detecting antibodies in the patient's serum that react to antigens–proteins that evoke an immune response–present in *Bb*. The existence of such antibodies indicates that a patient has probably been exposed to the Lyme pathogen.

The major deficiency of the Lyme ELISA is that it is not sensitive enough to the true antibodies of Lyme disease such as 23-25 kDa, 31 kDa, 34 kDa, 39 kDa and 83/93 kDa and over sensitive to 41 kDa, 45 kDa, 66 kDa antibodies that are seen in many non-Lyme situations such as periodontal disease.[19a]

Besides the problem of cross reactivity, there is still a problem of standardization; different labs that offer Lyme ELISAs vary in their results.[18]

To distinguish between false and true positives on ELISAs, physicians order a Western blot test, which looks at antibodies directed against a wide range of *Bb* proteins. In a patient having antibodies to a particular *Bb* protein, a "band" will form at a certain place on the immunoblot. By reading the "band" patterns formed by the spectrum of *Bb* antibodies, labs can determine with greater specificity whether a patient's immune response is specific for *Bb*.

Western blots contain two parts that detect two immuno-globins (antibody proteins), IgM and IgG; the IgM "band" pattern appears soon after infection, the IgG several weeks afterward, the latter sometimes peaking months or years later. Most immunoblot

---

[19] Coyle PK, Neurological Lyme disease *Semin Neurol* 1992;12:200-2008.

[19a] Harris, Nick, PhD, President IGeneX labs, Palo Alto CA, personal communication.

tests report these immunoglobin patterns separately, and the criteria for a positive result differ for IgM and IgG.

At a 1996 conference in Dearborn, MI, the CDC reduced the number of bands on the Western blot that it considers indicative of Lyme disease. Based on bands for Lyme showing most frequently on this test, the CDC criteria have since required five of ten bands for IgG and two of three for IgM. Note that the 1996 revision excludes bands for OspA and OspB, the 31kDa and 34kDa bands, respectively, which are very specific for Lyme.

Indirect antibody detection has limitations beyond those arising from the technology. Infected patients vary considerably from individual to individual in their serologic reactions to *Bb*.

In early Lyme, patients are expected to test negative because of the time it takes to develop detectable levels of antibodies.[3, 20] Up to half of patients with early Lyme can be negative in the first several weeks after infection. It can take up to four weeks before IgM antibody is measurable and up to eight weeks before IgG antibody is measurable.[3]

Patients treated with antibiotics during the early period of disseminated Lyme may have negative or equivocal serologies; the therapy presumably nullified their immune response.[3, 20] In other patients, antibodies may be detectable long after treatment, making it hard to distinguish between past or active illness. Also, recent research has shown that antibodies form complexes with antigens.[20] Currently marketed antibody tests can only detect free antibodies.

Detection of the *Bb* DNA through PCR assay and detection of pieces of the spirochete through antigen assays both give stronger indications of the presence of the Lyme pathogen; but currently, these tests don't conclusively prove that live *Bb* spirochete are present and causing active illness.[3, 21]

---

[20] Schutzer, SE et al, *Borrelia burgdorferi*-specific immune complexes in acute Lyme disease, *Journal of the American Medical Association* 1999;282:1942-46.

[21] Fallon BA et al, The underdiagnosis of neuropsychiatric Lyme disease in children and adults, *The Psychiatric Clinics of North America* 1998;21(3): 693-703.

Treatment

Diagnosed early, many cases of Lyme disease respond to short-term antibiotic therapy without recurrence. Optimal therapy for late Lyme, however, remains an unsettled question.[18] Identified in its late periods, Lyme appear less responsive to antibiotics, or appears to become manageable when antibiotics are given in repeated longer courses or for prolonged periods.

Typically, chronic Lyme patients are given an initial course of antibiotics, lasting for a month to six weeks. If a relapse occurs or symptoms persist, longer courses may be necessary. Certain "features" of the *Bb* spirochete suggest why: It has a slow growth rate, can remain dormant for lengthy periods, can invade intracellular sites, and may sequester in areas where antibiotic penetration is harder–for instance, the central nervous system, or the anterior chamber of the eye.[21]

Section four of the LDA *Update* on Lyme borreliosis is devoted to reports on the comparative efficacy of various antibiotics and modes of administering them in later-stage Lyme disease.

SCIENCE SECTION

Lyme Disease Update:
Science

LYME BORRELIOSIS:
DIAGNOSTIC DILEMMAS

This section of the *Lyme Disease Update* selectively digests, summarizes, or recommends published papers and articles concerned with diagnosing cases of persistent Lyme infection.

As the Overview to the *Update* indicates, diagnosing Lyme borreliosis is a complex, often uncertain process. A vast array of multisystem manifestations can be involved, with Lyme signs and symptoms in the early and later periods resembling the clinical manifestations of numerous other conditions. Also, with the exception of culturing live *Bb* spirochetes from the margins of the EM rash during early Lyme infection, which is not technically feasible, no corroborative test has been devised that is error-free.

Most of the papers included here devote substantial space to the problem of seronegativity and/or variable seroreactivity. Some focus on apparent improvements in detecting the presence of the *Bb* spirochete. Reflecting on the inadequacies of diagnostic tests for Lyme borreliosis, several commentaries urge more basic research on ways that the Lyme spirochete may elude immune detection and resist treatment.

Note: Papers published in European journals, when reporting on European cases, reflect differences between European and US strains of the Lyme pathogen.

PAPERS INVOLVING RELATIVELY LARGE NUMBERS OF PATIENTS DIGESTED IN THIS SECTION

The eight papers whose digests follow reported on patient groups numbering between 17 and 315 (counting clinical control groups). The earliest paper, published in 1988, helped establish the phenomenon of seronegativity in patients who develop chronic Lyme borreliosis after prompt antibiotic therapy believed to be usually effective.

Two papers, published in 1995 and 1996, reported on the detection of *B. burgdorferi* DNA in urine samples of patients though PCR tests. In the 1996 paper, a high percentage of the patients clinically diagnosed with persistent disease showed *Bb*-specific DNA in urine despite prolonged antibiotic treatment.

Three papers, published in 1990, 1994, and 1999, examined *Bb*-specific immune complexes during active Lyme infection. The aim in examining such complexes was to devise a simple technique to help confirm or rule out Lyme borreliosis in difficult-to-diagnose cases.

Dattwyler, RJ et al, Seronegative Lyme disease, *New England Journal of Medicine*, 1988; 319:1441-6.

Maiwald, M et al, Evaluation of the detection of *Borrelia burgdorferi* DNA in urine samples by PCR, *Infection* 23 (1995) No. 3:173-9.

Bayer, ME et al, *Borrelia burgdorferi* DNA in the urine of treated patients with chronic Lyme disease symptoms. A PCR study of 97 cases, *Infection* 24 (1996) No. 5:346-53.

Schutzer, SE et al, Sequestration of antibody to *Borrelia burgdorferi* in immune complexes in seronegative Lyme disease, *Lancet* 1990; 335:312-15.

Schutzer, SE et al, Early and specific antibody response to OspA in Lyme disease, *Journal of Clinical Investigation*, 1994; 94:454-57.

Schutzer, SE et al, *Borrelia burgdorferi*-specific immune complexes in acute Lyme disease, *JAMA*, 1999;282:1942-46.

DIGESTS

Dattwyler (1988)

In Dr. Raymond Dattwyler's 1988 *NEJM* study, he and his co-investigators sought to explain why some Lyme disease patients, though treated with oral antibiotics during the EM stage of infection, the early stage, continued to experience a variety of signs and symptoms. One hypothesis, Dattwyler et al remarked,

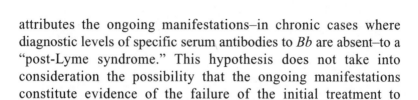

attributes the ongoing manifestations–in chronic cases where diagnostic levels of specific serum antibodies to *Bb* are absent–to a "post-Lyme syndrome." This hypothesis does not take into consideration the possibility that the ongoing manifestations constitute evidence of the failure of the initial treatment to eradicate the bulk of *B. burgdorferi* organisms.

For this investigation, the researchers selected 17 patients with clinically active, systemic Lyme borreliosis who lacked diagnostic levels of antibodies to *Bb* on either standard ELISA or IFA tests. (On Western blot tests, the level of seroreactivity against *Bb* in these patients was no greater than the level in normal controls.) They selected 18 patients from the same tick-endemic area with comparable manifestations and case histories who did show diagnostic levels of antibodies on ELISAs to serve as a positive control group. As a negative control, they selected 17 adults with no history of Lyme, rheumatic, or immune disease.

Since it was known that persons exposed to the Lyme pathogen develop a strong, sustained specific T-lymphocyte response prior to developing a measurable antibody response, Dattwyler et al used *Borrelia*-specific T-cell immune responses to document exposure to *Bb* in the 17 seronegative cases, finding a "vigorous" T-cell proliferative response in this group that was similar to the response in the positive control group: The T-cell responses in both groups of Lyme-infected subjects was stronger than the responses in the 17 healthy subjects.

Discussing their study, the investigators proposed that while early antibiotic therapy could have removed the etiologic agent from most sites of infection, Lyme spirochetes invading the CNS "and perhaps other privileged sites" may remain viable after standard treatment. They concluded:

"The presence of chronic Lyme disease cannot be excluded by the absence of antibodies against *B. burgdorferi* and that a specific T-cell blastogenic response to *B. burgdorferi* is evidence of infection in seronegative patients with clinical indications of chronic Lyme disease."

Maiwald (1995)

In a 1995 paper published in *Infection*, whose lead author was Dr. M. Maiwald, the researchers evaluated the reliability of PCR testing to detect *B. burgdorferi* DNA in cases where it is difficult to distinguish between previous and continuing infection. The accuracy of PCR tests becomes a critical issue when the effects of treatment require monitoring and the manifestations of Lyme borreliosis are not clearly distinguishable from signs and symptoms of other diseases.

The investigators took 114 urine samples from 74 patients: 51 samples from 26 patients with active Lyme; 36 samples from 27 patients with previous infection (showing no manifestations when their specimens were collected); and 27 samples from 21 seronegative control subjects without Lyme infection.

PCR assays gave the following results: Among the active cases, 25 urine samples from 17 patients showed *Bb* DNA, and 26 samples from this group tested negative. Among the asymptomatic cases in the second group, only one patient with previous infection showed a positive result. All the urine samples from the control subject were negative.

In conclusion, Maiwald et al observed that a positive PCR from urine has a high probability of indicating active Lyme borreliosis; on the other hand, the researchers noted, "as only 17 of the 26 patients with active infection were positive, a negative PCR result does not exclude active infection."

Bayer (1996)

Another paper utilizing PCR assays to detect the DNA of *Bb* spirochetes in urine samples from patients with chronic Lyme borreliosis appeared in *Infection* in 1996. The lead author was Dr. M.E. Bayer. This study, Bayer et al wrote, was prompted by the fact that only a portion of clinically-diagnosed patients meet criteria for serological confirmation of Lyme disease.

The researchers collected urine samples from 97 patients (selected by physicians), all of whom lived in the mid-eastern US and had presented with EM after an *Ixodes* tick bite. All had subsequently been given antibiotic therapy for extended periods of time, yet had continuing, often worsening Lyme-like signs and symptoms. The control group consisted of 62 healthy volunteers from the same geographic areas. Various medical specialists had asked Bayer et al to perform PCR tests to aid them in determining if Lyme spirochetes caused the manifestations in the chronically ill patients, or if an additional disease might be covering the Lyme manifestations with its own manifestations in these cases.

Using three primer pairs and three nested primers, the investigators searched for the presence of DNA sequences of the outer surface protein A (OspA) and of a chromosomal sequence of *B. burgdorferi*. Of the 97 patients, 72 (74.2%) showed positive PCRs, the rest had negative PCRs. All 62 people in the control group were PCR negative. In sum, the data from this study indicated that a high percentage of patients clinically-diagnosed with chronic Lyme may still excrete *Bb*-specific DNA–even after intensive antibiotic therapy.

Bayer et al ended their discussion with the following remarks: "Patients in the group studied here, including those of the PCR negative group, suffer from Lyme disease-like clinical symptoms which are difficult to distinguish from other diseases. A few of the patients in our study for whom recent serological data were available show an incomplete or negative serological profile for *B. burgdorferi* according to criteria of Western blotting. A further concern has arisen from the discovery that *B. burgdorferi*-positive patients may be also co-infected or superinfected with other tick-borne agents. Furthermore, currently uncultivable Borrelia species carried by a different tick (*Amblyomma americanum*) have been observed to cause a Lyme disease-like illness. These scenarios create a high degree of complexity of symptoms as well as the potential of an increased severity and duration of illness and heighten the consequences of a persistent presence of *B. burgdorferi* in the patient, a condition that would necessitate repeated broad-based laboratory testing and continued medical attention."

Schutzer (1990)

Spanning the 1990s, Dr. Steven Schutzer, working with different teams of co-investigators, published three reports prompted by diagnostic questions arising from *B. burgdorferi*-specific immune complexes (IC).

The first report, appearing in *The Lancet* in 1990, sought an explanation for seronegativity in cases where the EM rash went unobserved. It also sought to explain negative results in many instances in the main lab test for indirect detection of antibodies to *Bb*, the standard ELISA. Schutzer et al wondered if sequestration of antibodies in ICs could account for the apparent seronegativity in patients strongly suspected of having Lyme borreliosis. (Similar sequestration can occur, Schutzer et al pointed out, in hepatitis B, MS, systemic lupus, and syphilis.)

To examine this possibility, the researchers isolated and analyzed IC from 22 patients with signs and symptoms of Lyme disease who had tested negative on commercial ELISAs. (The process of isolating and analyzing IC for retesting involved a modification–the use of polyethylene glycol precipitation, abbreviated as PEG.) All subjects resided in two NJ counties endemic for *Ixodes* ticks. All but one had been treated with antibiotics prescribed by other doctors for a diagnosis other than Lyme. None had a history or evidence of immune deficiency, and none were under a recommended protocol for Lyme on entrance into the study. For their control groups, the investigators selected 22 seropositive patients with active Lyme borreliosis, and another 19 individuals from endemic areas, the latter including sero-negative patients with manifestations of other diseases and seronegative healthy persons.

IC samples from the 22 symptomatic seronegative patients were received in a blinded manner. The clinical histories were also unknown to Schutzer et al until all tests had been performed. Ten of these seronegative patients had an unequivocal history of EM, 12 had no history of the characteristic rash. The samples were then retested by ELISA to confirm the pre-study results indicating apparent seronegativity, and Western blots with relevant modifications were done to confirm the appearance of *Bb*-reactive antibodies which had been sequestered and thus not detectable before PEG-dissociation of the ICs.

Blinded analyses detected antibody to *Bb* in all ten sero-negative patients with EM, and in four of 12 seronegative patients who probably had Lyme disease but no history of EM. No antibodies were detectable in the 19 individuals comprising the second control group.

In discussing these findings, Schutzer et al proposed that their study showed that, "irrespective of the actual circulating concentration, the complexed antibody can be detected when simple techniques are used to isolate the complexes and dissociate antibody from its target antigen." With this in mind, the investigators added: "Complexed antibodies are likely to signify disease activity, whereas free antibodies alone do not necessarily do so."

Schutzer (1994)

Dr. Schutzer's next report on immune complexes appeared in the *Journal of Clinical Investigation* in 1994. Here the investigation focused on whether specific antibody to outer surface protein A (OspA) of the *B. burgdorferi* spirochete may form early in Lyme borreliosis but remain bound or at low levels in ICs.

For this 1994 paper, Schutzer et al took serum samples from 11 US patients with documented EM and 10 European patients with histories of EM. The control group consisted of 20 asymptomatic and otherwise healthy individuals, with no history of Lyme borreliosis, living in the same endemic US regions as the 11 American patients with Lyme.

Blinded analyses were again done for the serum samples. PEG-ELISAs were used to isolate and dissociate ICs. Biotin-avidin Western blot assays confirmed the ELISA results, while recombinant OspA was used to confirm antibody specificity. The analyses generated the following data: Specific complexed antibody to whole *B. burgdorferi* and recombinant OspA were detected in ten of 11 US EM cases, with IgM the predominant isotype to OspA. IgM isotype to OspA was detectable in all ten European cases with EM. These patients also had reactive T-cells to recombinant OspA. No specific complexed antibody was detectable in the 20 controls.

Summing up the implications of their research, the investigators stated that, "in humans, the ability to detect Ab [antibody] to OspA in the early weeks resolves part of a biologic puzzle." Further, Schutzer et al suggested, the "detection of specific Ab has important potential to support a clinical diagnosis in this illness, especially at the outset, when therapy is most likely to be effective."

Schutzer (1999)

Schutzer's third report, published in the *Journal of the American Medical Association* in 1999, supplied data suggesting the potential value of *B. burgdorferi* IC assays in support or exclusion of a diagnosis of Lyme borreliosis and as a possible marker of active infection.

This paper addressed the need for diagnostic lab tests to detect active Lyme disease, particularly in the roughly one-third of cases where the EM rash usually occurring in the early stage is not observed.

Emphasizing this need, the investigators noted that existing antibody tests for Lyme required a lag phase, often of several weeks, before showing positive results. They also note that in other infectious diseases the level of free antibody was not an adequate measure of active infection or recovery of health, whereas detection of complexed specific antibody more likely reflected active disease rather than a past exposure, for instance.

To obtain their data, Schutzer et al conducted a cross-sectional analysis of serum samples from a group of 168 patients meeting CDC surveillance criteria for Lyme borreliosis and a control group of 145 individuals, which included healthy persons and patients with other illnesses. Their analysis covered eight years. The main tests used to detect *Bb* ICs were the Lyme ELISA and Western blot, and all were performed blinded.

The researchers made the followings findings among the Lyme patients: *Bb* ICs were detected in 105 of 107 having EM who were seropositive; in 25 of 26 with EM who were early sero-negative; in 6 of 10 having culture-positive EM but were seronegative; in 13 of 13 patients with manifestations of neurologic Lyme without EM; and in 0 of 12 who had been treated for Lyme and had recovered. In the control group, only 2 of 50 patients with other diseases tested positive for ICs. All the rest were negative.

These results demonstrated, commented Schutzer et al, that formation of specific *Bb* ICs is a common process in active Lyme borreliosis, and that they can be detected by existing simple methods of antibody analysis.

Schutzer's published research in the 1990s progressed to where he and his colleagues had shown the following: Utilized adjunctively to detect complexed antibody, the chief diagnostic Lyme tests for indirectly detecting free antibodies were of potential value in confirming Lyme disease in the early stage—especially when a substantial percentage of patients do not present with EM and where prompt appropriate treatment can prevent the development of acute or chronic illness.

SMALL OR SINGLE CASE STUDIES SUMMARIZED IN THIS SECTION

Eight small studies (less than ten subjects) or single case reports are summarized in this part of the section on diagnostic dilemmas in Lyme borreliosis. Concerned primarily with late disease, all appeared in peer-reviewed journals between 1989 and 1998.

In general, these eight papers have been selected because they illustrate equivocal aspects of persistent Lyme infection, especially Lyme's tendency to mimic the symptoms and signs of other diseases and the problems of false negative serology and varying seroreactivity.

Two studies utilized PCR analyses to look for evidence of *B. burgdorferi* DNA or spirochetal antigens in joints, synovial fluid, and synovial membranes—possible sites at which *Bb* may elude antibiotic therapy and host immune response. One study, evaluating four patients, suggested in some instances that the current methods of treatment are incapable of completely eradicating the *Bb* spirochete and stopping the pathogenic process. If so, long-term IV antibiotic therapy, with its greater risks and expense, would be the only expedient for preventing irreversible damage. Several six-case series reported on isolating *B. burgdorferi* from CSF and skin biopsies (including the first iris biopsy), many months after antibiotic therapy.

Another report, on one patient, is offered as an example of an all too common problem in Lyme borreliosis—a patient who returns to premorbid status despite early diagnosis of infection. Yet another single case report raised the possibility that chronic Lyme infection may exacerbate previous or concurrent immunologic illness.

Note again: Studies appearing in European journals, involving European patients, deal with strains of the Lyme pathogen that may differ from US strains in biology, manifestations, and response to antibiotic treatment.

SUMMARIES

Petrovic, M, et al, Lyme borreliosis; a review of the late stages and treatment of four cases. *Acta Clinica Belgica*, 1998; 53.3; pp. 178-83.

The cases included two males, two females, their ages ranging from 12 to 40. The purpose of the review was to illustrate aspects of late Lyme borreliosis, the problem of false negative serology, and the necessity of long-term antibiotic therapy in chronic or recurrent disease. All four patients had medical histories and symptoms and signs suggesting Lyme disease.

In the first patient, initial neurological, ELISA, and PCR tests came back negative. The researchers reanalyzed the samples after a new test became commercially available, the Enzygnost ELISA, which has a high sensitivity for IgM antibodies. The new results proved positive for IgM, weakly positive for IgG. Western blot testing confirmed the results. The researchers regarded the positive serology and the clinical evolution after antibiotic therapy as "post hoc proof" that this patient had Lyme borreliosis. (His symptoms first appeared in May 1995. By Jan. 1996 he had become asymptomatic.)

The second patient, a man, recalled tick bites and skin lesions suggestive of EM. Enzygnost ELISA showed positive for IgM, weakly so for IgG, and immunoblot confirmed these results. Given doxycycline for five weeks, his arthralgia, fatigue, and myalgia eased, then reappeared two weeks after this antibiotic regimen ended. When re-administration of doxycycline for six weeks showed no improvement, he was given ceftriaxone daily for three weeks, which completely resolved his general manifestations. But three weeks later, arthralgia of the knees and myalgia in both legs recurred. A control Enzygnost ELISA was unchanged. At this point, he was placed on a regimen for refractory Lyme borreliosis (ceftriaxone, six weeks, followed by oral cefadroxil for 100 days). The patient's manifestations resolved and he remained nearly asymptomatic.

Patient three, a man, had been diagnosed with tuberculous meningitis in the summer of 1995 and put on a six-month regimen of pyrazinamide, isoniazid, and rifampicin. The manifestations persisted, and he had trouble working. In Feb. 1996, he suffered an epileptic seizure and doctors reconsidered his case, performing various tests, including an Enzygnost ELISA which proved strongly positive for IgG and negative for IgM. During a medical history taken at this time, he recollected a tick bite before the first clinical signs and symptoms appeared in 1994 and skin lesions suggestive of EM which developed two weeks later. The doctors now diagnosed neuroborreliosis with chronic meningo-encephalopolyradiculitis and treated the patient with ceftriaxone for three weeks. The general manifestations vanished, although he continued to have difficulty walking.

The fourth patient, a young girl, had developed a skin lesion on her belly resembling EM after returning from a vacation in a plateau region where *Ixodes* ticks are endemic. The lesion resolved spontaneously. Several weeks later, she presented with diminished muscular strength, particularly in her arms, and was diagnosed at first with polyradiculoneuritis, based largely on clinical manifestations and electromyography. When Enzygnost ELISA and immunoblot tests showed positive for *B. burgdorferi*, she was rediagnosed with polyradiculoneuritis caused by *Bb*, and given ceftriaxone IV daily for three weeks, followed by oral cefadroxil for 100 days. The manifestations completely regressed.

Priem, S, et al, Detection of *Borrelia burgdorferi* by polymerase chain reaction in synovial membrane, but not in synovial fluid from patients with persisting Lyme arthritis after antibiotic therapy. *Ann Rheum Dis* 1998;57:118-21.

Priem et al investigated four patients; a 50-year-old male and three females ranging in age from 51 to 28. They were accepted for this study based on the following criteria: All resided in an area highly endemic for Lyme borreliosis. All had typical monarthritis or oligoarthritis affecting the knees, which had not responded to treatment. Further, they had a positive serological test for Lyme arthritis, in accordance with CDC surveillance standards, and reactive arthritis or collagen vascular disease could be found in each one. There was no clinical or serological evidence for other inflammatory rheumatic illness, including rheumatoid arthritis. The researchers addressed the following concerns: the tendency for Lyme arthritis to mimic other rheumatalogical conditions; the difficulty in interpreting chronic cases where patients show an isolated IgG seropositivity that does not discriminate between past or active infection; and the even greater difficulty in attributing clinical manifestations to persistent infection with *B. burgdorferi* when patients suffer ongoing or recurring manifestations after antibiotic treatment.

The objective of this study was to identify possible sites of bacterial persistence in these four patients. The researchers chose the PCR test to detect *Bb* DNA in the synovial membranes (SM) of the patients when PCR results from synovial fluid (SF) became negative after antibiotic therapy. In the PCR testing, the investigators looked at paired SF and SM specimens and urine samples, using primer sets specific for the OspA gene and a p66 gene of *Bb*.

At the time of presentation for this investigation, after cessation of antibiotic therapy eight to ten weeks earlier, and all four patients were still seropositive for *B. burgdorferi*, all still had active arthritis. The reseachers collected urine samples, then within one week obtained parallel SF and SM specimens. PCR analyses detected no *Bb* DNA in the urine and SF samples. In contrast, the SM samples were PCR positive. Patients one and two showed positive with OspA primer, patient three with p66 primer only; SM samples from patient four were PCR positive with both primer sets. Because of these PCR findings and the persisting arthritis, the patients were again given antibiotic treatment. Patients one, two, and four received cefotaxime for three weeks, followed by six weeks of oral doxycycline or minocycline, respectively. Patient three received imipenem for two weeks, followed by doxycycline for six weeks. In all four patients, the arthritis "completely subsided" within four to six months and did not recur after a median observation period of 18 months.

The investigators concluded: "Taken together, this study shows that in patients with ongoing or recurring Lyme arthritis after antibiotic therapy a negative *B. burgdorferi* PCR in SF or urine does not necessarily exclude a persisting infection. In these patients, SM biopsy specimens should be obtained for PCR analysis, which is much more sensitive than SF PCR to detect intraarticular persistence of the bacterial DNA. This is important because [SM] PCR positive patients are likely to suffer from ongoing infection and therefore may benefit from additional antibiotic therapy."

Liegner, KB, et al, Lyme disease and the clinical spectrum of antibiotic responsive chronic meningoencephalomyelitides. Journal of Spirochetal and Tick-borne Diseases, Fall/Winter 1997, pp. 61-73.

Liegner et al intensively studied four patients with chronic inflammation of the meninges, brain, and spinal cord believed to be caused by Lyme borreliosis. Their investigation revealed persistent infection and seronegativity and/or variable seroreactivity as the common threads. Their evaluation of the response to treatment in these complex "cryptic" cases required the use of all known methods (in the mid-1990s) over a prolonged period of time.

The first patient, a 39-year-old woman, had resided in a NY county endemic for ticks and in northern California but recalled no tick bites or EM. In 1975, she had been diagnosed with idiopathic thrombocytopenic purpura (ITP) and had undergone a splenectomy the next year. Beginning in 1989, she was reevaluated after a two-year history of cranial nerve palsies, persistent unexplained cerebral spinal fluid (CSF) pleocytosis, and progressive spastic quadraparesis. Prior to a proven diagnosis for Lyme borreliosis, she manifested clinical disease for at least four years. Numerous times throughout this patient's illness, lab evidence for chronic persistent infection was developed, which included culture, repeated PCR positivity, and demonstration of spirochetal-compatible forms in pericardial biopsy—all despite prior, some-times protracted IV antibiotic treatment. The patient also showed markers for lupus erythematosus; however, corticoid therapy for systemic lupus produced severe clinical deterioration. Only after six months of daily IV antibiotic treatment did she dramatically improve. Whenever treatment was discontinued, though, she relapsed, presumably due to previous neurologic damage.

Patient two, an outdoorsman living in NY's Catskill Mts., was 61-years-old when he developed a large round rash on his thigh in the autumn of 1985. He consulted a physician, who provided no treatment. The following winter, this patient developed constant headache, low-grade fever, paresthesias, and truncal instability. Lumbar puncture showed lymphocytic pleocytosis, and an ELISA for Lyme was negative. When dysphasia and a progressive stroke syndrome manifested, he was diagnosed with vasculitis and treated with cyclophosphamide and steroids for a number of months. He deteriorated progressively to a functional level slightly above a persistent vegetative state. A Lyme ELISA was positive in 1988. He then received IM ceftriaxone (CFTRX) for two weeks, which resulted in slight improvement. A CAT scan in 1992, revealed massive hydrocephalus, an electroencephalogram revealed status epilepticus, so phenobarbital was prescribed. At this point, with various diagnostic tests showing conflicting or varied sero-reactivity, the patient was treated with daily IV CFTRX for a month, then weekly cefotaxime (CFOTX) for a year. This regimen modestly improved his neurological state.

He succumbed to his illness in July 1993, and autopsy disclosed ependymitis, florid meningoencephalomyelitis, and severe hydrocephalus. Lab tests showed his CSF positive for OspA antigen and Lyme-specific immune complexes. Electron micro-scope study visualized *Borrelia*-compatible structures in formalin-fixed tissues. His brain tissue and dura matter were PCR positive for *B. burgdorferi*-specific oligonucleotides.

In the case of the third patient, a 37-year-old woman who removed a tiny tick from her shin while visiting Dutchess County in the spring of 1982, multisystem manifestations appeared within months. (*Ixodes* ticks are plentiful in this NY area.) An eruption at the site of attachment, lasting until 1987, was biopsied and read as granuloma annulare. Several Lyme ELISAs between 1982 and 1990 were negative. When neurologic signs and symptoms manifested in the summer of 1993, serologic tests were negative for Lyme borreliosis in serum and CSF," as was CSF culture for *B. burgdorferi*, and OspA antigen in CSF, and PCR and Lyme-specific immune complexes in CSF and serum."

For the next eight months, the patient was treated with daily IV CFOTX, and the last three of five CSF samplings during CFOTX therapy revealed Lyme-specific immune complexes. Western blots now demonstrated key *Bb* bands. From July 1994 through 1997 (the year this study was published), the patient was maintained on weekly IM benzathine penicillin, combined with azithromycin, and remained clinically well. Two Western blots in 1996 showed numerous bands indicative of Lyme. Lyme ELISAs between 1982 and 1995 were all negative–a period of 13 years.

Case four, a 40-year-old man whose clinical history began in Oct. 1989, illustrates the capability of Lyme borreliosis to "mimic" the signs and symptoms of many other conditions. He could recall no deer tick attachments, there was no history of EM, but he did remember a large tick attachment while on the coast of SC, followed by joint manifestations. He had also spent considerable time in shore areas of CT, MA, and RI (known habitats of *Ixodes* ticks).

Initially, he developed optic neuritis, experienced constitutional symptoms, and manifested progressive neurologic symptomology believed to be multiple sclerosis (MS) on clinical grounds. Despite treatment for MS, which included beta interferon, he deteriorated to a wheelchair-bound status. In view of his lack of response to MS therapy, an empirical treatment, daily CFOTX, was tried between the fall of 1994 and spring, 1995. The patient's neurologic status reversed, enabling him to walk 100 feet without aid. His movements also became more fluid and his speech clearer. MRI and CSF examination confirmed improvement. But Western blots in April and May (1995), though not fully diagnostic, indicated evolution of key *B. burgdorferi* bands. Also for the first time, Lyme-specific immune complexes were seen in serum. OspA antigen in CSF remained negative.

Treated with IM benzathine penicillin combined with azithromycin, the patient again lost the ability to walk and developed bladder and bowel incontinence. Lumbar puncture five months after discontinuation of this antibiotic regimen again suggested MS. Antibiotics were given intravenously at this juncture, and he regained ambulatory ability and bladder and bowel control. Lumbar puncture in March 1996 confirmed significant improvement in CSF parameters, and Lyme-specific IgM immune complexes were detectable in the CSF.

Discussing the fourth case, Liegner et al pointed to a significant body of research data amassed in pre-WWII Germany concerning a possible relationship between spirochetal infection and MS. They called for additional studies using modern direct antigen detection techniques to reexamine this potential relationship.

In conclusion, Liegner et al offered analogies between Lyme borreliosis and other spirichetal diseases, particularly syphilis– specifically: There is precedence in such illness for seronegativity and chronic persistence, both accepted phenomena today in syphilis. More clinicians are turning to prolonged combined antibiotic therapy to avert progressive neurosyphilis, under a hypothesis that in syphilis total eradication of the etiologic agent may not be possible.

They added: "Relapses following uses of potent antibiotics and detection of the Lyme organism or its DNA following treatment likewise demonstrate an inability to completely eradicate the pathogen and permanently halt the pathologic process with current methods of treatment in some patients. This is a problematic situation because intensive antibiotic treatment is costly, is inconvenient, and carries associated risk for the patient. Such antibiotic usage may foster the emergence of strains of other types of bacteria resistant to the antibiotics employed and thus has public health implications. For such patients, however, this may be the only presently available alternative to progressive neurologic deterioration."

Nanagara, R, et al, Ultrastructural demonstration of spirochetal antigens in synovial fluid and synovial membrane in chronic Lyme disease: possible factors contributing to persistence of organisms. *Human Pathology*, Oct. 1996, pp. 1025-34.

This systematic study (the first of its kind), used electron microscopy (EM) and immunoelectron microscopy (IEM) to demonstrate ultrastructural pathological changes and the presence of spirochetal antigens in the synovial membrane (SM) and synovial fluid (SF) cells of patients with chronic Lyme arthritis. Eight male patients, ranging between 8 and 67 in age, were included in this study. The total duration of arthritis ranged between two months to three years, but the most recent episode or exacerbation in each patient was six weeks. All had experienced recurrent exacerbations in the arthritic joint under study before a definite diagnosis had been made. Five also had other system involvement at the early stage of the disease before arthritis occurred. Six had oligo- or polyarthritis, the knee joint being the most common joint involved. Treatment before arthrocentesis and/or biopsies were performed included systemic corticosteroids in three patients (two patients for neurologic and cardiac manifestations before arthritis, the other in combination with oral azathioprine for concurrent pemphigus). Four patients had treatment with intra-articular corticosteroid injections, one of whom suffered repeated arthritis attacks shortly after each injection. Three had previous treatment with antibiotics, but only one of these received long-term antibiotics.

EM examinations were done on eight SF samples and four SM specimens obtained by percutaneous needle biopsy. IEM examinations were done on three SF samples and one SM biopsy, using monoclonal antibody to *B. burgdorferi* OspA as the immunoprobe to detect the presence of *Bb* spirochetes. IEM identified *Borrelia*-like structures in all four SM specimens. EM found such structures in two of eight SF samples. Prominent ultrastructural findings included signs of vascular injury in acute and also chronic Lyme synovium, and fibrin and proteinaceous-like materials within subsynovial areas apparently correlated with sites showing vascular changes.

Taking together the EM and IEM findings in this study, the researchers concluded: "Electron microscopy adds further evidence for persistence of spirochetal antigens in the joint in chronic Lyme disease. Locations of spirochetes or spirochetal antigens both intracellularly and extracellularly in deep synovial connective tissue as reported here suggest sites at which spirochetes may elude human host response and antibiotic treatment."

Goldings, AS, Neuroborreliosis in Texas. *Journal of Spirochetal and Tick-borne Diseases,* Sept. 1995, pp. 59-61.

Goldings reported on a case of neuroborreliosis in Texas as an "all-too-common" clinical problem, a patient who returns to premorbid status despite early recognition of infection. She also addressed issues of seronegativity, "particularly as they apply to regions of the country where strain variation of *Borrelia* is expected and its influence on standardized testing is unknown." (Texas, she explains, is an endemic area for Lyme borreliosis, but *B. burgdorferi* has been isolated from the black-legged tick [*Ixodes scapularis*], the brown dog tick [*Rhipicephalus sanguines*], the cat flea [*Ctenophalidis felix*], and a recently-identified vector, the "lone star tick" [*Amblyomma americanum*].)

The patient, a perfectly healthy 28-year-old man until May 1992, presented with EM associated with tick attachment, a virus-like illness, and documented aseptic meningitis with Bell's Palsy. He also had secondary skin lesions consistent with hematogenous spread. Correctly diagnosed, he was treated for one week with IV antibiotics, then oral antibiotics for three weeks. (At the time Goldings case study was published, 1995, appropriate IV antibiotic therapy to effect bacteriological cure in Lyme meningitis had increased to three to four weeks.)

Half a year later, he showed dysfunction of the fifth cranial nerve, and two months after that dysfunction of the eighth cranial nerve (signs of mononeuritis multiplex, a known complication of Lyme infection). Severe pain developed in the frontotemporal area associated with chills, nausea, night sweats, and vertigo. Hospitalized with a fever of 101°F, he was tested for antibodies to Ehrlichia, HIV, leptospira, and Lyme, with negative results. Repeat CSF to detect Lyme antibody or other signs of abnormality was negative, and a lesion in the left parietal white matter seen on a previous MRI was not seen on a repeat MRI. His doctors suspected he had a new febrile illness, perhaps viral, with associated vascular headaches and labyrinthitis. After several more months of chronic fatigue and continuing headaches and night sweats, he again sought medical help, received no treatment, but was "told to return as necessary."

A few months later–20 months after the tick bite–he consulted his physicians yet again. Headaches and severe joint pains had forced him to quit work. He found himself confused, fatigued, forgetful, unable to concentrate. A bedside examination showed cognitive impairment. A lumber puncture was remarkable for a protein of 50. Both CSF examination for Lyme antigen and PCR were negative. When six weeks of oral antibiotics failed to improve the patient, he was given IV cefotaxime twice a day for a month, which did reduce the confusion and fatigue. Efforts to then withdraw him from therapy were accompanied by subjective worsening, so he was maintained on oral antibiotics.

One year later he complained of worsened neuropsychiatric manifestations. Neuropsychology tests confirmed cognitive impairment, and he received pulse therapy with cefotaxime three days per week over a six-week span. Goldings followed his case a month longer, at which time his headaches, joint aches, and muscle pains improved subjectively, while cognitive difficulties continued. In her discussion of this case, she remarked: "It is possible that the first physician either did not know that relapses can occur with LD and retreatment is necessary, failed to suspect that the neurological complications were related to LD, or simply assumed ensuing symptoms were not due to LD because of seronegativity. Some degree of physician latitude is expected in assessing the need for retreatment, but criteria are not well defined. Unfortunately current laboratory testing [as of 1995] may not always confirm the disease and therefore may mislead the uninformed physician."

Preac-Mursic, V, et al, First isolation of *Borrelia burgdorferi* from an iris biopsy. *Journal of Clinical Neuro-ophthalmology*, Vol 13, No 3, 1993, pp. 155-61

This case study reported on the isolation of *B. burgdorferi* from six patients; from four CSF samples, from a biopsy of an EM rash, and from an iris biopsy–the first time *Bb* had been isolated from the iris of a human eye. The patients had been diagnosed with Lyme borreliosis mostly by clinical signs. Three patients were male, 17, 25, and 60 years-old. Three were female, 24, 55, and 62 years-old.

Clinical and microbial findings included the following data: Five patients manifested ocular disorders. (Preac-Mursic et al noted that the published Lyme literature contained reports of conjunctivitis, keratitis, iritis, uveitis, vitritis, endophthalmitis, ischemic optic neuropathy, optic neuritis, oculomotor palsy, and retinal vasculitis.) Serological tests for IgM antibodies to *Bb* were negative in all six. For IgG antibodies, four were positive, two negative. All had been treated with antibiotics. In two cases, corticosteroids had been given for the ocular conditions.

Examination of the CSF samples and iris and skin biopsies was done by darkfield microscopy and by culture in MKP medium. Identification of the isolates was done by Western blot with *Bb*-specific monoclonal antibodies. The researchers used an indirect immunofluorescence test (IFT) to determine antibodies in serum and CSF.

Preac-Mursic et al commented in their discussion of this case study: "Characteristic of Lyme borreliosis is that its clinical picture is rarely complete and symptoms are overlapping, which makes diagnosis more difficult. A *Borrelial* infection is usually confirmed by determining *B. burgdorferi* antibodies. However, interpretation of serological tests and results may not be straightforward. False-positive and false-negative results occur. Negative serological results do not necessarily exclude *Borrelia* infection. As shown here and previously reported, antibiotic therapy may abrogate the antibody response to the infection, but *B. burgdorferi* may persist. In clinically unclear cases, much greater significance is therefore attached to the isolation of *B. burgdorferi*.

We were able to isolate *B. burgdorferi* from CSF and skin biopsies months to years after the antibiotic therapy and disappearance of Erythema migrans. The lack of repeated insect bite and Erythema migrans, negative AB-titers against *B. burgdorferi* and negative CSF examination suggest persistence of the lack of *B. burgdorferi* rather than reinfection."

Fraser, DD, et al, Molecular detection of persistent
***Borrelia burgdorferi* in a man with dermatomyositis.**
***Clinical and Experimental Rheumatology* 10: 387-90, 1992**

Fraser et al reported on a case of a 40-year-old man previously diagnosed with immunologic disorders, including dermatitis herpetiformis and anti-Jo-1 autoantibody-positive dermatomyositis, who subsequently developed clinical Lyme borreliosis. Prompting them to present this case history was their inability to find a report of a patient with pre-existing immunologic illness who later became infected with Lyme.

The patient, who lived in an area endemic for *Ixodes* ticks, was seen in May 1989 manifesting EM and symptoms and signs compatible with early Lyme disease. He remembered being bitten by a tick at the center of the expanding rash two weeks before the onset of manifestations. At the time, he was receiving cytotoxic therapy for his immunologic conditions and had been in stable health for several months.

Soon after he presented, the patient's serum protein electrophoresis demonstrated elevated levels of immunoglobins and oligoclonal banding. He was diagnosed with acute Lyme borreliosis. Lyme titers and blood and urine samples were obtained. All cytotoxic treatment was discontinued, but he was maintained on daily oral prednisone.

Initially, the patient was given IV ceftazidine, which appeared to worsen the manifestations in a way consistent with a Jarisch-Herxheimer reaction, and oral tetracycline was given instead for two weeks, producing no adverse effect. Twice during this period, his serum Lyme titers were negative.

In June, his weakness, rash, and fever increased. The next month, more oral steroids were prescribed and high-dose IV methotrexate (with leukovorin rescue biweekly) was reinstituted. In Sept., because of a chronic leg ulcer and associated cellulitis, he started taking oral Keflex, which was changed over the next month to tetracycline and then to erythromycin because of what were thought to be allergic rashes. By October, his illness responded completely, his serum Lyme titer was negative, and the interval between methotrexate doses was lengthened as his serum creatine kinase normalized.

In January, 1990, when the patient again complained of growing weakness, oral chlorambucil was added to his treatment regimen, while monthly IV methotrexate was continued. Several months later, persistent Lyme borreliosis was diagnosed by PCR testing of his peripheral blood leukocytes for *Borrelia* DNA. All serologic, T-cell stimulation, and Western blot analyses, however, were negative. The patient responded to long-term oral antibiotics (ampicillin), probenicid therapy, and concurrent cytotoxic treatment. Subsequent PCR testing of the patient's leukocytes has been repeatedly negative for *B. burgdorferi*.

Fraser et al concluded: "This case suggests a role for chronic *Borrelia* infection in the exacerbation of immunologic disease and demonstrates the usefulness of PCR in assessing sero-negative Lyme disease in immunocompromised patients".

Preac-Mursic, V, et al, Survival of *Borrelia burgdorferi* in antibiotically treated patients with Lyme borreliosis. *Infection,* 17 (1989) Nr 6, pp. 355-59.

In a case series involving six patients, Preac-Mursic et al demonstrated the persistence of *Bb* in skin and CFS after treatment with antibiotics and the disappearance of EM.

The subjects included four males, ranging from 5 to 49 years in age, and two females, 26 and 60 years of age. Half had been diagnosed with the early stage sign, EM, the other half with Bannwarth's Syndrome (encephalitic and meningeal symptoms characteristic of later Lyme).

Antibody titers in blood for IgG and IgM were measured for five patients. Three showed borderline levels for IgG. For IgM, one patient showed borderline levels, a second showed significantly elevated levels. The researchers determined serum antibody by IFT.

B. burgdorferi spirochetes were isolated in all cases from three CSF samples and three skin biopsies, between one and three months after therapy from biopsy, and between 3 and 7 months after therapy from CSF. The investigators examined the skin and CSF specimens by darkfield microscopy and MKP medium (see Preac-Mursic et al's paper, 1993, above, for reference to this medium).

ADDITIONAL READING

Liegner, KB, Lyme disease: the sensible pursuit of answers. *Journal of Clinical Microbiology*, Aug. 1993; pp. 1961-63

In this guest commentary, published in 1993, Dr. Liegner noted that researchers are just "beginning to clarify" how it is possible for a bacterial infection to resist powerful antibiotic therapy. In support, he cites scientific observations on intracellular localization of *Borrelia burgdorferi* within macrophages, within fibroblasts, and within human umbilical vein endothelial cells *in vitro*. In the first and second instances, researchers were able to recover or culture *B. burgdorferi* from macrophages and fibroblasts after antibiotic treatment. In this connection, Liegner also referred to a contemporaneous editorial pointing out that infections caused by intracellular pathogens are "notoriously" difficult to cure. These observations, he adds, "lead one to the conclusions that certain subsets of patients with Lyme disease may require prolonged antibiotic treatment."

Turning to a major difficulty in diagnosing Lyme, seronegative laboratory test results, Liegner then made the following outright statement: "Many clinicians and scientists admit that seronegative Lyme disease exists but maintain that it is a rare phenomenon. Indeed, for study purposes, many academic centers have specifically excluded patients presenting with symptoms possibly compatible with Lyme disease who are seronegative."

Leigner suggested that this is a "serious conceptual and methodologic error," considering the current rudimentary knowledge of how the human immune system responds to Lyme infection. He then gave several examples of poorly-understood immune responses in Lyme, ending with mention of research on circulating immune complexes which indicates that "in patients for which a state of antigen excess exists" free antibodies may elude detection and only be revealed after "use of methods to dissociate such immune complexes."

Liegner concluded: "Thus, the very patients who are unable to generate detectable levels of free antibodies, who are least apt to contain the infection, and who may present with the most serious illness among those with Lyme disease are least likely to be offered treatment."

Donta, ST, Lyme disease: a clinical challenge. *Journal of Spirochetal and Tick-borne Diseases,* Sept. 1995; pp. 50-51

Dr. Donta, in a special editorial published in 1995, addressed problems in diagnosis and treatment of Lyme borreliosis. Concerning attempts to solidify the clinical diagnosis of Lyme disease using serologic methods, he remarks that these attempts "are simply inadequate with current methodology." Further, he called it "syllogistically illogical to conclude with what has already been reported that a positive serology defines, and a negative serology excludes, Lyme disease."

As evidence for this position, Donta detailed well known inadequacies of both the ELISA and Western blot tests and summarized the plusses and minuses of PCR-DNA analyses of blood, urine, and cerebrospinal fluid. The role of PCR analysis in diagnosing Lyme, he said, "remains to be delineated."

In conclusion, Donta expressed the hope that, "as with any disease in which information is incomplete and evolving, our energies can be directed toward improving our understanding of Lyme disease through more research into the pathogenesis and treatment of the illness."

Wahlberg, P, et al, Treatment of late Lyme borreliosis. *Journal of Infection* (1994), 29, 255-61.

NEUROBORRELIOSIS

Lyme borreliosis, a multisystem, multiphase illness, often invades the central nervous system (CNS), causing neurologic and psychiatric disorders. Up to 40% of symptomatic Lyme disease cases manifest neurologic or psychiatric signs and symptoms.[1]

Early Lyme neurologic conditions include cranial neuritis, encephalitis, meningitis, and radiculoneuropathies. In later Lyme disease (chronic or recurrent), patients may develop encephalo-myelitis and encephalopathy. Psychiatric manifestations associated with Lyme include bipolar disorder, dementia, major depression, obsessive-compulsive disorder, panic attacks, paranoia, and schizophrenia.[2]

Because the multiple manifestations of neurologic and neuropsychiatric Lyme borreliosis mimic those of a myriad of other known conditions, even Lyme specialists may find it hard to distinguish Lyme from these other diseases. Failure to distinguish Lyme neuroborreliosis from other neurologic and psychogenic disorders, however, can result in inappropriate care and progression to a chronic state that only partly or temporarily responds to proper treatment.

The papers, reports, and studies selected for this section of the *Lyme Disease Update* offer scientific evidence aimed at better acquainting physicians and others involved in the care of patients with the complex and often confounding neurologic and neuropsychiatric aspects of Lyme disease.

---

[1] Tager FA et al, Psychiatric and cognitive features of Lyme disease, *Psychiatric Annals*, 2001;31, No. 3: J2-J11. Also: Reik L, Lyme disease and the nervous system. New York:Thieme;1991.

[2] Fallon BA et al, The neuropsychiatric manifestations of Lyme borreliosis, *Psychiatric Quarterly*, 1992;63, No. 1:95-117.

ARTICLES ON LYME NEUROBORRELIOSIS DIGESTED IN THIS SECTION

Logigian, EL et al, Chronic neurologic manifestations of Lyme disease, *The New England Journal of Medicine,* 1990;323:1438-44.

Pfister, H-W et al, Randomized comparison of ceftriaxone and cefotaxime in Lyme borreliosis, *The Journal of Infectious Diseases*, 1991;163:311-18.

Fallon, BA et al, The neuropsychiatric manifestations of Lyme borreliosis, *Psychiatric Quarterly*, 1992;63, No. 1:95-117.

Fallon, BA et al, Lyme disease: a neuropsychiatric illness, *The American Journal of Psychiatry*, 1994;151:1571-83.

Trieb, J et al, Clinical and serologic follow-up in patients with neuroborreliosis, *Neurology*, 1998;51:1489-91.

Fikrig E et al, Preferential presence of decorin-binding protein B (BBA25) and BBA50 antibodies in cerebrospinal fluid of patients with neurologic Lyme disease, *Journal of Clinical Microbiology*, Mar. 2004:1243-46.

DIGESTS

Logigian (1990)

In the US, EM, the skin lesion characteristic of early Lyme borreliosis was first reported in 1970. Lyme arthritis was first reported as a separate rheumatic condition in 1977. The bacterial organism responsible for Lyme infection was first identified in 1981. And in 1987 and 1989, two chronic neurologic syndromes associated with Lyme disease were described, one involving the peripheral nervous system and the other involving the central nervous system. In some instances, however, the evidence connecting these neurologic syndromes to infection by the *Bb* spirochete was incomplete. In 1990, a paper on chronic neurological manifestations of Lyme disease appeared in *The New England Journal of Medicine*, reporting on a study of 27 patients in whom chronic neurologic syndromes had developed from three months to

14 years after the onset of Lyme. The lead author was Dr. Eric L. Logigian. Dr. Allen C. Steere, the research clinician who had "discovered" Lyme arthritis, was a co-author.

Logigian et al conducted this study to define further the chronic neurologic abnormalities of Lyme borreliosis. The patients chosen as subjects, ranging from 25 to 72 years of age, had previous signs of *Bb* infection, current evidence of immunologic reactivity to *Bb*, and chronic neurologic manifestations with no other attributable cause. Three neurological syndromes emerged, alone or in combination: encephalopathy, polyneuropathy, and leukoencephalitis–the latter an inflammation of the white matter of the brain. In some cases, these syndromes emerged after lengthy periods of latency, as in neurosyphilis.

Summarizing the results: 24 patients (89%) showed a mild encephalopathy, characterized by memory loss, mood changes, or sleep disturbances. Of these, 14 had memory impairment in neuropsychological testing, and 18 showed increased CSF protein levels, evidence of intrathecal production of antibodies to *Bb*, or both. Nineteen patients (70%) had polyneuropathy with either distal paresthesias or radicular pain; 17 of these also experienced encephalopathy. Electrophysiologic tests revealed axonal poly-neuropathy in 16 patients. One patient had leukoencephalitis marked by asymmetric spastic diplegia, intrathecal production of antibodies to *Bb*, and periventricular lesions in the white matter. Among the full patient group, associated signs and symptoms included: fatigue (74%), headache (48%), arthritis (37%), and hearing loss (15%).

Six months after treatment with a 2-week course of IV ceftriaxone, 17 patients (63%) had improved; 10 patients (37%) had improved and then relapsed, or evidenced no improvement. Discussing their study, the investigators concluded: "The typical response of our patients to antibiotic therapy supports the role of spirochetal infection in the pathogenesis of each of the syndromes described here. However, our results were not as good as those in previous reports. Six months after treatment, more than one-third of the patients either had relapsed or were no better. In addition, more than half had previously received antibiotic therapy thought to be appropriate for their stage of disease and still had progression of the illness. The likely reason for relapse is failure to eradicate the spirochete completely with a two-week course of intravenous ceftriaxone therapy. On the other hand, the patients who did not improve may have had irreversible damage to the nervous system, particularly since the response to therapy tended to be worse in patients with longer duration of disease. This is reminiscent of far-advanced neurosyphilis, in which the response to penicillin may be minimal."

Pfister (1991)

By the mid- and late-1980s, a relative handful of studies had already been published on the susceptibility of various strains of *Bb* to different antibiotics. Those reports suggested that treatment with cefotaxime and ceftriaxone appeared effective. A randomized comparison of the two antibiotics in Lyme neuroborreliosis was published in 1991. Its lead author was Dr. Hans-Walter Pfister. In addition to determining comparative efficacy, Pfister et al sought to determine CSF minimal inhibitory concentrations (MIC) for the two drugs.

They conducted a prospective, randomized, open study, entering 33 patients with Lyme neuroborreliosis; 17 were randomly assigned to 10-day IV treatment with ceftriaxone, 16 were assigned to 10-day IV treatment with cefotaxime. Thirty of these patients, suffering from Lyme meningitis and painful Lyme radiculoneuritis (called Bannwarth's syndrome in Europe), proved eligible for analysis of therapeutic efficacy. CSF antibiotic concentrations were above the MIC 90 level for *Bb* in almost all patients.

The results disclosed no clinical differences between the two groups during treatment or at follow-up. Clinical improvement was seen 3-5 days into therapy for most patients. Neurologic manifestations improved or subsided in 14 patients on cefotaxime and in 12 on ceftriaxone during treatment. Evaluation after 8.1 months (mean) showed 17 of 27 patients had become clinically asymptomatic. In one patient, *Bb* was isolated from CSF 7.5 months after ceftriaxone. Noting that 10 patients remained symptomatic at follow-up and *Bb* persisted in the CSF of one patient, Pfister et al concluded: "a prolongation of therapy may be necessary."

Fallon (1992)

As the two articles reviewed above established, by the early 1990s, physicians were increasingly recognizing the neurologic manifestations of Lyme borreliosis and evaluating antibiotic regimens for comparative effectiveness. The neuropsychiatric presentations of Lyme disease and the treatments of choice, however, were not well known.

In 1992, *Psychiatric Quarterly* published an article that shed light specifically on the neuropsychiatric aspects of Lyme. This article consisted of two sections: the first, an overview of Lyme borreliosis and a thoroughly-referenced review of the pertinent neuropsychiatric literature; the second, a discussion of problems that typically confront patients having Lyme neuroborreliosis–which included detailed clinical "vignettes" based on data from some 200 patients with seropositive Lyme. The second section also offered guidelines to help clinicians working with such patients. Dr. Brian A. Fallon, the lead author of the article, was credited with putting together the overview. The discussion and guidelines were credited to psychiatrist Jenifer A. Nields, a co-author.

Fallon remarked in a foreword to the overview that psychiatrists have been aware that CNS infections can be responsible for severe psychiatric illness, since the cause of syphilis was identified early in the 20th century. Similarly, they have been aware that prompt antibiotic therapy may prevent permanent neurologic damage. He then proceeded to cover the following areas concerning Lyme disease: diagnosis, distribution, history, clinical profile (the lengthiest part), lab tests, treatment, and psychiatric manifestations.

Dr. Nields' discussion of Lyme neuroborreliosis "phenomenology" encompassed fatigue and memory loss (94% and 83% of patients sampled, respectively), photophobia (70%), sensory hyperacusis (48% abnormalities of sound, 30% of taste, 23% of smell), extreme irritability and/or emotional lability (84%), word reversals in speaking and/or letter reversals in writing (69%), spatial disorientation (57%), fluctuations in manifestations (no percentage given), worsening of manifestations during antibiotic therapy (nearly 50%), and uncertainty regarding diagnosis and treatment (no percentage given).

Proposing guidelines for psychiatrists and considering the patient's perspective on the clinical experience of Lyme, Dr. Nields concluded: "From the foregoing clinical vignettes, it should be clear that Lyme disease, particularly when it involves the central nervous system, can in some patients be an extremely debilitating, bizarre, terrifying and perplexing disease. It can present in a great variety of ways, and the symptoms can fluctuate dramatically and unpredictably. At the same time, there are patterns to its emergence that can suggest the diagnosis where laboratory indices are inconclusive. Much uncertainty surrounds the diagnosis and treatment of Lyme disease at this stage of its history, and such uncertainty adds to the distress that the illness causes for patients. Lyme disease is aptly called the "new great imitator," and it can imitate psychiatric disorders no less than medical ones. Psychiatrists working in endemic areas are well advised, then, to keep Lyme disease in mind as part of their differential diagnosis for a broad range of disorders...especially in cases that are atypical or otherwise suggestive of systemic disease. It should be borne in mind also that new clinical manifestations of Lyme disease are still being discovered and described."

Fallon (1994)

Drs. Brian Fallon and Jenifer Nields again published a review of the books, articles, and abstracts from academic conferences concerning the neuropsychiatric manifestations of Lyme borreliosis in 1994. Appearing in *The American Journal of Psychiatry*, this article, primarily aiming to familiarize more psychiatrists with Lyme, emphasized the "biological substrate" of the neuropsy-chiatric manifestations associated with this disease. The spectrum of such syndromes, they explained, was just beginning to be elucidated in the medical literature. Concurrently, biological research and brain-imaging techniques were indicating a psychological basis for the neuropsychiatric signs and symptoms through several mechanisms: direct infection in the CNS; specific, localized autoimmune reactions; or centrally active immunological responses to systemic infection.

Fallon and Nields added a number of sections to this later overview, consistent with its emphasis on the biology of *Bb*. (Their previous article had accorded equal space to the patient's perspective–the secondary emotional reactions to Lyme which relate to particular aspects of its manifestations.)

Additionally included was a brief discussion of the CDC criteria for diagnosis, since Lyme disease had become nationally reportable in 1991. Fallon and Nields agreed that those criteria had proven useful for epidemiological studies, but they found shortcomings in the CDC case definition: about a third of patients never recalled an EM rash; serologic tests remained unreliable; most critical, the clinical spectrum of Lyme borreliosis was continuing to expand beyond signs and symptoms required by the CDC definition.

A new short section compared Lyme with syphilis. After detailing numerous similarities, it called attention to the following key differences: *T. pallidum* (syphilis) is generally transmitted from host to host. A vector transmits the Lyme spirochete. Peripheral neuropathy and radiculopathy are common in Lyme. Syphilis does not share these features.

Taking into consideration the most recent biological findings, Fallon and Nields also included an extensive section on the microbiology of *Bb*. Here they listed features understood to factor into an organism's ability to resist standard periods of antibiotic therapy–genetic variability, intracellular location, long replication time, and sequestration in hard-to-penetrate sites. *Bb* seems to exhibit all these characteristics.

Re: genetic variability. Fallon and Nields mentioned animal research indicating that *Bb* spirochetes alter genetically after sequestration in the CNS, resulting in a new strain that differs from the strain of the infecting peripheral spirochetes; such strain variation, they suggested, may have produced the differences between the presentation of Lyme in the US and its presentation in Europe.

Another recent finding brought out in the microbiology section: *Bb* spirochetes have been observed shedding blebs (membranous material) during growth. Researchers hypothesized that in some cases these blebs may bind all free circulating *Bb*-specific IgM antibodies, enabling the microorganism itself to elude immune surveillance. Further discovery that the blebs have potent, non-specific mitogenic activity has led researchers to hypothesize that this activity may inappropriately and ineffectively stimulate the immune system, initiating autoimmune disease processes.

The last section in this paper projected future directions in research. Fallon and Nields specified two major areas of clinical significance where knowledge about Lyme borreliosis was lacking: diagnosis, and the optimal treatment for persistent conditions. On the latter, they stated: "Definitive treatment guidelines for Lyme disease have not been established because knowledge about this illness continues to evolve"; however, as studies had shown that *Bb* can rapidly invade the CNS, they recommended aggressive treatment as early as possible.

Trieb (1998)

One paper that pursued data on optimal treatment for persistent Lyme borreliosis subsequent to Fallon and Nields' 1994 article should be concisely digested here before passing onto the summaries of small cases series. *Neurology* published this paper in 1998. The lead author was Dr. J. Trieb. Trieb et al performed a clinical and serological follow-up study of 44 patients with signs of neuroborreliosis and specific intrathecal antibody production. The study group had been culled from 6,775 clinic patients tested by IgG ELISA for *Bb*. All 44 patients had been treated with ceftriaxone for 10 days. The follow-up exams were carried out 1.2 to 4.2 years after antibiotic therapy.

From the follow-ups, the investigators learned that although neurologic deficits had decreased significantly, more than half the patients had unspecific complaints resembling a chronic fatigue syndrome. More than half also showed persisting IgM serum titers for *Bb* in Western blots. Considering the persistence of clinical manifestations and serologic markers in a large number of patients, Trieb et al raised the possibility of improving the long-term clinical outcome by either a single more protracted course of therapy or a second course.

Fikrig (2004)

Dr. Patricia Coyle, a neurologist at the SUNY, Stony Brook, and Dr. Steven Schutzer, University of Medicine and Dentistry of New Jersey (UMDNJ), were co-investigators in this study. Schutzer's research on immune complexes appears in the diagnostic section of this *Update.*

Discussing the data obtained from this study, Fikrig et al pointed out that "these data provide the first description of differential immunoscreening to identify *B. burgdorferi* antibodies that may be preferentially expressed in the CNS."

Dr. Brian Fallon, the lead author in several papers in this section on neuroborreliosis, contributed the following appraisal:

"Fikrig et al.report on a study which examined whether the gene expression of the Borrelia burgdorferi spirochete is different in the CSF than in the serum. Probing a *Bb* expression library with CSF and sera from patients with neurologic Lyme disease, the phage clones that selectively reacted with CSF were isolated and then the genes were expressed in recombinant form, allowing for the use of a specific antibody ELISA.

"IgG or IgM antibody responses were detectable against two proteins (BBA25 and BBA50) in CSF but not serum, indicating preferential antibody production during neuroborreliosis. The strongest CSF antibody response–13 of 22 patients with neurologic Lyme disease developed CSF IgG–was against BBA25 (decorin-binding protein B), a protein that facilitates the attachment of spirochetes to glial cells, suggesting a role in pathogenesis.

"This study demonstrated once again that *Bb* gene expression varies depending upon specific location, be it the mid-gut of the tick, the salivary gland of the tick, or in the skin, joints, or heart of the human. This is the first time, however, that spirochete gene expression in the CNS has been shown to differ from gene expression in other tissues.

"Equally important, this study demonstrates the power of a new technique to identify previously unrecognized antibody responses in the CSF against *Bb*, thus leading to new insights into pathogenesis and new CSF assays to diagnose neurologic Lyme disease."

SMALL CASE STUDIES SUMMARIZED IN THIS SECTION

Two small case series and a single case report are summarized below. The first series included seven patients with neuro-borreliosis who also experienced lower urinary tract dysfunction. (At the time of publication, 1993, very limited data on bladder dysfunction or urodynamic findings associated with Lyme disease had appeared in the literature.) The single case history, a postmortem report of a case of rapidly progressive dementia and marked subcortical degeneration attributable to the presence of *Bb*, was the first report (to the authors' knowledge) of a clinico-pathologic investigation of dementia in Lyme disease. The second case series, evaluating three cases, illustrated that while Lyme disease may be overdiagnosed in rheumatology clinics, in psychiatry clinics for children and adults it may go under-diagnosed.

SUMMARIES

Chancellor, MB et al, Urinary dysfunction in Lyme disease, *The Journal of Urology*, 1993;149:26-30

This paper studied 3 men and 4 women with confirmed Lyme borreliosis 1 week to 8 months prior to urological evaluation. The men ranged from 33 to 68 years of age, the women from 19 to 63.

Diagnosis had been based on clinical signs, neurological symptoms lasting more than 3 months unattributable to other illness, evidence of cellular or humoral immunity to *Bb*, decreased Lyme antibody titers after antibiotics, and the agreement of infectious disease and neurology consultants on the diagnosis. The patients had presented with a variety of neurological manifestations, including paraparesis with partial sensory loss. One patient, a 68-year-old man, had temporarily been in a coma. According to the first table in this paper, none of the patients had a history of tick bite, and only two had EM within 3 months of the onset of neurological manifestations.

Among the observations made by Chancellor et al, nocturia, urge incontinence, and urinary urgency were the most common urological signs. Patients commonly suffered relapses, at a rate similar to relapse rates previously reported. In half the patients who had received antibiotic treatment believed appropriate, the illness still progressed. In all patients, neurological and urological manifestations resolved slowly, and convalescence was protracted.

These observations suggested that the Lyme spirochete may directly invade the urinary tract, and therefore voiding dysfunction may be part of neuroborreliosis. As a possible explanation for the relapses, the researchers pointed to failure of the usual 2-week course of IV ceftriaxone therapy to eradicate the spirochete completely. In endemic areas, Chancellor et al concluded, "Lyme disease must be included in the differential diagnosis of voiding dysfunction."

Waniek, C et al, Rapidly progressive frontal-type dementia associated with Lyme disease, *Journal of Neuropsychiatry,* 1995;7:345-47

Waniek et al reported on the case of a man who succumbed to neuropsychiatric Lyme in his early 50s. He had lived in an area where Lyme disease was endemic; however, because the onset of illness, when he was in his late 40s was atypical, with psychiatric manifestations only, the possibility of Lyme borreliosis was not considered until very late – when the patient finally showed positive antibody titers.

Given IV antibiotics for 4 weeks, followed by oral antibiotics for another 6 weeks, the patient improved significantly. After 5 months, he relapsed. At this point, he had a negative antibody titer, had been treated with antibiotics on the presumption of Lyme, and was showing clinical signs consistent with a mild dementia syndrome.

Transferred to several state hospitals, where Lyme disease was no longer considered, and thus no additional antibiotic treatment given, his dementia progressed. His cognitive function and judgment declined dramatically. His memory was grossly impaired, his concentration span extremely short. He became totally disoriented, incontinent, and mute. Ultimately, he died of aspiration pneumonia.

Discussing this case, Waniek et al assumed that the brain damage was due to Lyme borreliosis, noting that the morphology of the spirochetes found in the thalamus region upon neuro-pathologic examination was consistent with *Bb*. Also, the brain lesions were quite different from those of other spirochetal infections. This report raised an important clinical issue: A diagnosis of Lyme disease should be considered even in cases presenting as purely psychiatric. Longer antibiotic therapy should be considered as well.

Fallon, BA et al, The underdiagnosis of neuropsychiatric Lyme disease in children and adults, *The Psychiatric Clinics of North America*, 1998;21, No. 3:693-703

The authors opened this article by offering evidence from the research literature of "underdiagnosis" of Lyme borreliosis, especially when patients present with manifestations that appear to be primarily neuropsychiatric. They devoted the mid-part of their article to a review of typical clinical manifestations of Lyme disease and the existing diagnostic "tools" to support the diagnosis of Lyme. They ended with case studies of 3 patients initially diagnosed with different conditions: attention deficit disorder (ADD), depression, and multiple sclerosis (MS).

Case 1, a girl residing in a Lyme endemic area, developed problems focusing in class at age 7 and was diagnosed by a neuropsychologist with probable ADD. When a Lyme ELISA done during a comprehensive medical work-up showed positive, she was re-diagnosed with Lyme and treated with antibiotics. The treatment resolved her "ADD," but for the next 2 years she remained antibiotic-dependent. At 9, she was able to come off antibiotics, and for 3 years she was symptom-free. At 12, she relapsed, and serologic tests revealed a positive ELISA and Western blots with fully reactive IgG and IgM. On a mental status examination, she qualified for a diagnosis of attention deficit hyperactivity disorder (ADHD). Additional cognitive tests led to a diagnosis of persistent encephalopathy secondary to Lyme. Treated subsequently with oral antibiotics for several months, the patient regained her previous level of health. At the time of publication, she remained with no signs of her prior ADHD symptoms.

Long-standing depression had been diagnosed in the second case, a 16-year-old boy living in an endemic area, who recalled embedded tick bites but no EM rash and had quit sports in the 7th grade because of painful knees. His grades had declined in most courses since the 8th grade. Asked on presentation about his physical and cognitive status, he acknowledged numerous physical complaints and cognitive problems.

Considering his suspicious clinical history, further testing was done, and his IgG Western blot revealed 4 Lyme-specific bands, although 2 Lyme ELISAs in the prior 3 months had shown negative. Neuropsychologic tests indicated deficits in processing speed and visual spatial memory. A brain SPECT supplied findings consistent with encephalitis, vasculitis, and Lyme borreliosis. Rediagnosed with probable Lyme encephalopathy, he received 12 weeks of IV ceftriaxone, which gave excellent cognitive, emotional, and physical results. No longer depressed, the patient improved his school performance markedly, and follow-up testing showed a rise of 22 full-scale IQ points.

Patient 3, also residing in a Lyme endemic region, was twice bitten by ticks at 39. Shortly after, he developed an array of neurologic manifestations. Serologic tests were unremarkable, and some CSF studies were normal or nonreactive, but his CSF had an abnormal WBC and mildly elevated myelin basic protein. A neurologist diagnosed transverse myelitis, secondary to presumed seronegative Lyme, and put him on IM ceftriaxone for 2 weeks, followed by oral doxycycline for 4 weeks, which relieved his headaches. After that, the patient received oral prednisone, which resolved his leg weakness and foot drag. Nevertheless, over the next 5 years, many signs and symptoms, including headaches, persisted with no clear cause.

At 44, he began experiencing diffuse multisystemic manifestations. Various tests were again ordered. His CSF appeared normal; but neurologic exams, a brain MRI, and nerve and eye studies disclosed abnormalities. Despite the normal CSF, he was now diagnosed clinically with MS and treated with prednisone, which improved only his vision and energy.

A year later, he presented with the same diffuse multisystemic complaints. Most of his lab tests were within normal limits; however, Lyme serologies included a Western blot positive for IgG, while a brain SPECT indicated continuing abnormalities, notably decreased perfusion diffusely throughout the cortex, the white matter, and the basal ganglia bilaterally. This time, the diagnosis was changed to Lyme disease–without excluding concurrent MS.

For the following 9 months, the patient was taken off steroids and treated with high dosages of oral cefuroxime and minocycline, which improved his condition, enabling him to return to work. At one point, his left-sided paresthesias and weakness returned, prompting a repeat MRI that pictured a worsening of demyelination of his brainstem. The antibiotics were switched to IV ceftriaxone and clarithromycin for 12 months. Serial MRIs showed diminution of white matter lesions, and no new ones. Based on responsiveness to the antibiotics, serologies, and history, both his infectious disease physicians and his neurologist changed this patient's diagnosis from MS to a resolving antibiotic-responsive Lyme encephalomyelitis.

ADDITIONAL READING

Pachner, AB et al, *Borrelia burgdorferi* infection in the brain: characterization of the organism and response to antibiotics and immune sera in the mouse model, *Neurology* 1990;40:1535-40

In this study, Pachner et al utilized mice, since the white-footed field mouse is a natural reservoir for *Bb* in the wilds of the US. Further, researchers had already established in the mouse model that the bladder, kidney, and spleen readily become infected after inoculation.

Focusing instead on the brain, the investigators sought to determine if *Bb* could be cultured from the brain as easily as from other organs. They also sought to analyze the distribution of organ infection after inoculation with the Lyme spirochete and to document the spirochete's ability to affect the brain directly. Additionally, they studied a brain isolate by analysis of its plasmid DNA and the *in vitro* response to immune human sera and mouse sera.

Pachner et al noted that all over the world, Lyme borreliosis most commonly presented in the nervous system; how *Bb* damaged the nervous system, though, was still poorly elucidated. Moreover, they emphasized, while this question was clinically important, it had proven difficult or impossible to investigate in human patients.

These experiments in the murine model indicated the following: *Bb* is neurotropic. Analysis of extrachromosomal DNA showed that a brain isolate can differ from the original infecting strain. The *Bb* spirochete appears relatively insensitive to the effects of immune sera; and only by prolonged incubation with relatively large doses of antibiotics can it be killed *in vitro*. Another noteworthy finding, regarding immune response: The evidence suggested that active infection, not dead antigenic material, was necessary for continued stimulation of an immune response and maintenance of high antibody titers.

Tager FA et al, A controlled study of cognitive deficits in children with Chronic Lyme disease, *The Journal of Neuropsychiatry and Clinical Neurosciences,* 2001; 13:500-507

This study sought more information about long-term neurologic sequelae that may manifest in children as cognitive dysfunction. Previous studies have shown that such dysfunction occurs in adults with chronic neurologic Lyme.

Twenty children, ranging in age from 8 to 16 years, with a history of new-onset cognitive complaints after Lyme were enrolled and matched against 20 healthy children. Various measures of cognition and psychopathology were used to assess each child.

The results indicated that children with Lyme experienced significantly more cognitive and psychiatric disturbances. Further, after controlling for anxiety, depression, and fatigue, cognitive deficits still manifested in the Lyme cases. Tager et al concluded: "Lyme disease in children may be accompanied by long-term neuropsychiatric disturbances, resulting in psychosocial and academic impairments."

In their discussion, the investigators noted: "These findings are important because children with [Lyme disease] who present with psychiatric problems may be misdiagnosed as having a primary psychiatric problem such as an affective disorder, oppositional defiant disorder, or attention deficit disorder."

ATYPICAL FORMS
OF BORRELIA BURGDORFERI

The scientific literature on Lyme borreliosis includes a "wealth of reports" about the survival of *Borrelia burgdorferi*, the spirochete infecting humans with Lyme disease, after lengthy or repeated antibiotic treatment.[1]

This literature also includes observations of the *Bb* spirochete transforming into cystic structures under various conditions, mostly *in vitro* (during laboratory experiments).[2]

The papers digested and recommended in this section on persistent Lyme borreliosis are reports on atypical forms of *Bb* examined both *in vitro* and *in vivo* (in live organisms). The primary objective of these studies was to investigate whether the changes in spirochetal structure seen *in vitro* might be occurring in patients, and, if they were, whether these *in vivo* alterations might "explain why *Borrelia* infection can be temporarily dormant, why a reactivation of the disease may occur when the conditions suit *B. burgdorferi*, and why the infection may relapse after treatment with antibiotics."[3]

An attendant or related concern of several of the papers here is the difficulty in conclusively confirming a diagnosis of Lyme borreliosis. The chief laboratory "tools" for confirmation–direct cultivation of viable spirochetes, PCR analysis of *Bb* DNA, indirect

---

[1] Brorson, O et al, A rapid method for generating cystic forms of *Borrelia burgdorferi*, and their reversal to mobile spirochetes, *APMIS*, 106(1998): 1131-41.

[2] Preac-Mursic, V et al, Formation and cultivation of *Borrelia burgdorferi* spheroplast-L-form variants, *Infection* 24 (1996); No. 3:218-26. Also: Brorson, O et al, Transformation of cystic forms of *Borrelia burgdorferi* to normal, mobile spirochetes, *Infection* 25 (1997); No. 4:240-45. And: Alban, PS et al, Serum-starvation-induced changes in protein synthesis and morphology of *Borrelia burgdorferi*, *Microbiology* (2000), 146:119-27.

[3] Brorson, O et al, Transformation of cystic forms of *Borrelia burgdorferi* to normal, mobile spirochetes, *Infection* 25 (1997); No. 4:240-45.

detection of antibodies by serology–all have shortcomings, with false positives and false negatives frequent.[4]

The most conclusive ways to diagnose Lyme disease developed to date, directly detect the *Bb* microorganism by cultivation or through visualization by a sophisticated type of electron microscope. In most of the papers that follow, the researchers utilized these methods, particularly the latter, to make their findings. Note: The papers in European journals on European *Borrelia* usually discuss strains of the Lyme pathogen differing biologically from US strains.

ARTICLES ON ATYPICAL FORMS OF *Bb* DIGESTED IN THIS SECTION

MacDonald, AB et al, Clinical implications of delayed growth of the Lyme borreliosis spirochete, *Borrelia burgdorferi*, *Acta Tropica*, 48(1991)89-94.

Schaller, M et al, Ultrastructure *Borrelia burgdorferi* after exposure to benzylpenicillin, *Infection* 22 (1994); No. 6:401-06.

Kersten, A et al, Effects of penicillin, ceftriaxone, and doxycycline on morphology of *Borrelia burgdorferi*, *Antimicrobial Agents and Chemotherapy*, 39 (1995); Vol. 5:1127-33.

Preac-Mursic, V et al, Formation and cultivation of *Borrelia burgdorferi* Spheroplast-L-form variants, *Infection* 24 (1996); No. 3:218-26.

Aberer, E et al, Heterogeneity of *Borrelia burgdorferi* in the skin, *American Journal of Dermatopathology* 18(6):571-79, 1996.

Brorson, O et al, Transformation of cystic forms of *Borrelia burgdorferi* to normal, mobile spirochetes, *Infection* 25 (1997); No. 4:240-45.

---

[4] Brorson, O et al, A rapid method for generating cystic forms of *Borrelia burgdorferi*, and their reversal to mobile spirochetes, *APMIS*, 106(1998): 1131-41.

Brorson, O et al, In vitro conversion of *Borrelia burgdorferi* to cystic forms in spinal fluid and transformation to mobile spirochetes by incubation in BSK-H-medium, *Infection* 26 (1998); No. 3:144-50.

Brorson, O et al, A rapid method for generating cystic forms of *Borrelia burgdorferi*, and their reversal to mobile spirochetes, *APMIS*, 106(1998): 1131-41.

Alban, PS et al, Serum-starvation-induced changes in protein synthesis and morphology of *Borrelia burgdorferi*, *Microbiology* (2000), 146:119-27.

DIGESTS

MacDonald (1991)

A report appearing in *Acta Tropica* in 1991, whose lead author was Dr. Alan B. MacDonald, looked into the clinical implications of delayed growth of the *Bb* spirochete. Two unsettled questions underlay this study: Why in some cases does Lyme borreliosis become clinically active after a prolonged latent period? Why do some patients with active Lyme suffer clinical relapses after antibiotic therapy?

Seeking clues, MacDonald et al investigated the possibility that cultivation of biopsy specimens from EM for periods up to 1 year might reveal strains of *Bb* whose cells divide very slowly. They reasoned that if such slow-growth strains could be found, that would suggest why some *Bb* spirochetes may survive in hosts for lengthy periods of time.

Selecting 63 patients from an endemic Lyme area in Long Island, NY, the researchers examined *in vitro* cultures of biopsies from the active edge of EM patches. The examination of each culture tube was done by darkfield microscopy beginning 3 weeks after inoculation, then repeated at monthly intervals. Examinations continued until they detected spirochetes or 12 months had elapsed.

Bb spirochetes were recovered after protracted incubation of skin biopsies from 16 patients with EM. Detection of motile spirochetes ranged between 2.5 and 10.5 months. The average time period was 181 days (6 months).

In discussing their report, MacDonald et al noted: "Antibiotics are only able to kill actively dividing *Borrelia*. If a *Borrelial* cell does not divide at least once during the period of antibiotic therapy, it may persist in the host and produce relapse or recrudescence of the disease." Therefore, the abstract of this paper concluded: "Some patients with Lyme borreliosis may require more than the currently recommended 2 to 3 week course of antibiotic therapy to eradicate strains of the spirochete which grow slowly."

Schaller (1994)

In 1994, *Infection* published a paper reporting on changes in the ultrastructure of *Bb*. The morphological alterations were induced through exposure of *Bb* to increasing concentrations of benzyl-penicillin. The lead author was Dr. M. Schaller. At the time of publication, researchers had no precise knowledge about these changes.

To examine the morphological effects, the investigators obtained skin samples by biopsy from EM lesions, isolating and subcultivating the *Borreliae* in a modified BSK-II medium. For 5 days, the isolates were exposed to increasing concentrations of penicillin G. Using the broth dilution method, the in vitro minimum inhibitory concentration (MIC) for a *B. burgdorferi* skin isolate was determined to be 0.5 mg (the lowest concentration of penicillin at which no growth occurred).

After 5 days incubation, the cultures were examined by darkfield microscopy for the presence of motile spirochetes. Electron microscopy was used to observe ultrastructural changes in spirochetes exposed to antibiotics. As a control, the morphological structure of spirochetes not exposed to penicillin was also observed by electron microscopy.

Schaller et al found the following alterations: 1. At 0.0625 mg, many outer sheath blebs; 2. at 0.125 mg, total loss of the outer sheath and a characteristic irregular waveform of the *Borrelial* cells; 3. at the same concentration, the presence of "spheroplasts"; 4. Again at a concentration of 0.125 mg, an irregular pattern of structural changes in the protoplasmic cylinder complex; 5. At 0.25 mg and 0.5 mg, disruption of the cylinder complex into several parts; 6. at 1 mg and 2 mg, severe cytolysis.

Kersten (1995)

Antimicrobial Agents and Chemotherapy published a report in 1995 on the effects of antibiotics on the morphology of *Bb*. Specifically, the antibiotics under investigation were penicillin, ceftriaxone, and doxycycline. Dr. A. Kersten was the lead author.

Taking note that the survival of Lyme spirochetes in the tissues of some patients after seemingly adequate antibiotic therapy might be responsible for the late complications and chronic course of Lyme borreliosis, and noting also that *Borreliae* (or parts of them) appear to withdraw into sites where they are further inaccessible to antibiotics, Kersten et al questioned whether "antibiotics themselves can be made responsible for transforming the organism into a persistent, viable, or nonviable but antigenically potent form."

For a clearer understanding of how *Bb* may persist after antibiotic treatment, the researchers investigated the different modes of degeneration of *Bb* suspensions during a 4-day exposure to antibiotic solutions. Observations of ultrastructural changes in the suspensions during the exposure period were made by darkfield microscopy. Visualizations of spirochetal parts after exposure to all three antibiotics were done by transmission electron microscopy. Darkfield microscopy showed increased blebbing and the gradual formation of granular and cystic structures. Motile organisms were still present after incubation with penicillin and doxycycline but not after ceftriaxone. Under transmission electron microscopy, intact spirochetal parts, mostly situated in cysts, were seen up to 4 days after exposure to all antibiotics.

Considering experiences from studies with other spirochetes, e.g., syphilis, the investigators suggested that "encysted *Borreliae*, granules, and the remaining blebs might be responsible for the ongoing antigenic stimulus leading to complaints of chronic Lyme borreliosis." In discussion, Kersten et al rephrased the implications of their findings: "The exposure of *Borrelia* cultures to antibiotics in vitro for 96 h cannot be compared with the actions of antibiotics given for two or more weeks in vivo. Morphologically intact *Borrelia* parts seen after 4 days of incubation with antibiotics, however, may also persist in humans during antibiotic treatment."

Preac-Mursic (1996)

Why *B. burgdorferi* persists in some patients despite adequate antibiotic therapy was the question addressed again in a paper appearing in *Infection* in 1996. The lead author of this paper was Professor Vera Preac-Mursic. Here, the researchers conducted *in vitro* investigations of morphological variants and atypical forms of *Bb* in order to learn more about the variation in the 3 genospecies of *Bb* and to elucidate the role of atypical forms in Lyme borreliosis.

Bb strains examined in this study were isolated from human CSF, skin biopsies, and blood by culture in MKP medium after incubation for 2-15 weeks. The *Borreliae* isolates came from antibiotically-treated and untreated patients, who had been clinically diagnosed with definite or probable Lyme disease, and from patient specimens contaminated with bacteria. Analysis of the isolates during exposure to penicillin G *in vitro* was also undertaken.

Darkfield microscopy and scanning electron microscopy showed diverse changes. "Persisters" isolated from 60-80% of the treated patients had an atypical form. Morphological changes in culture with penicillin G gradually developed, increasing with duration of incubation. Pleomorphism, the presence of elongated forms and spherical structures, an inability of cells to replicate, a long period of adaptation to growth in MKP medium, and mycoplasma-like colonies after growth in solid medium were all observed, suggesting that Lyme spirochetes produce spheroplast L-form variants.

These variants without cell walls, Preac Mursic et al offered, could explain why *Borrelia* survive so long in the organism "and the cell-wall-dependent antibody titers disappear and emerge after reversion."

Aberer (1996)

Two unsatisfactorily-resolved problems in research on Lyme borreliosis prompted a study of the heterogeneity of *Bb* in the skin. The report on this study, whose lead author was Dr. E. Aberer, appeared in *The American Journal of Dermatopathology* in 1996. The first problem involved diagnosis. Partly because of the unreliability of *in vitro* methods to confirm *Bb* infection, diagnoses of Lyme disease were still frequently being based on clinical grounds alone. The second problem involved how the tissue-bound *Bb* spirochetes induced clinicopathological change. At the time of publication, this process had not been sufficiently defined.

Aberer et al conducted their study to determine where Lyme *Borreliae* were situated, their morphology, and the number actually observable in diseased skin. To deal with the small size of *Bb*, which limits utilization of conventional microscopy, they turned to a videomicroscope. (Videomicroscopy magnifies 2,000 times, permits tracing of stained structures over their full length, including extensions into surrounding tissues, and "pictures" on a monitor the 3-dimensional shape of stained structures.)

Skin biopsies from patients with EM, ACA, and morphea provided specimens for examination. These were stained with the "*Borrelia* genus-specific flagellar antibody H9724." The investigators identified *Borrelial* structures in all three specimen types. Images obtained from skin tissues were then compared and found identical to *Borrelial* shapes seen in culture fluids, agar-embedded *Borreliae*, *Bb* exposed to antibodies or antisera, and *Borreliae* in a *Borrelia*-injected skin model.

From their findings, Aberer et al drew a number of conclusions, one central: "The H9724-reactive structures represent various forms of *B. burgdorferi* rather than staining artifacts."

Three other conclusions drawn by the researchers: (1) Video-microscopy clearly offers a reliable technique for identification of *Borrelia* in situ. (2) *Borreliae* may escape immune surveillance by colony formation and masking within collagen, resulting in seronegativity. (3) Determining that *Bb* can be morphologically diverse has provided insights into the large spectrum of *Bb*–associated diseases and also given indications of a heterogenous immune response in individuals.

Brorson (1997)

The transformation of cystic forms of *Borrelia burgdorferi* into normal, mobile spirochetes under controlled conditions was the subject of a report published in *Infection* in 1997. The lead author in this evaluation was Dr. O Brorson. The researchers reviewed what had been learned to date. Encysted forms of *Bb* had been seen in tissues. The same phenomenon had occurred *in vitro* due to the spirochetes being exposed to antibiotics, changes in pH, aging, and depletion of metabolites. Two crucial unanswered questions: Were these atypical forms low metabolic *Bb* states that could transform later to a normal state? Were they degenerated, dead bacteria?

Seeking clues, Brorson et al cultivated *Bb* in a commercial medium, without serum, where *Bb* only multiplied slowly, changing into encysted forms after 1 week. These cysts were then transferred to the same culture medium, but with rabbit serum added to the medium. Within 6 weeks, the encysted forms changed back into regular mobile *Bb* spirochetes, and their regeneration time was normal. Examination by transmission electron microscope revealed transverse fission inside the cysts.

In their discussion, the researchers commented: "These cystic forms seem to be an alternate morphologic state to which *B. burgdorferi* resorts when the environment becomes too unfavorable. In our study the unfavorable conditions were created by a culture medium (BSK-H) which was too scanty because of the absence of rabbit serum. From the electron microscopical observations it appears that the encysted forms of *B. burgdorferi* arise because of bacterial fission."

They added in conclusion: "In vivo these encysted forms may explain why *Borrelia* infection can be temporarily dormant, why a reactivation of the disease may occur when the conditions suit *B. burgdorferi*, and why the infection may relapse after treatment with antibiotics."

Brorson (1998)

Infection published another report by Brorson et al in 1998, once more on the conversion of *Bb* to cystic forms, except this time the research focused on the estimated 11% of Lyme disease patients who experience neurological signs and symptoms.

Noting that detection of antibodies in CSF was the usual method of confirming a diagnosis of neuroboreliosis, and that cultivation of *Bb* from CSF was the most convincing method for revealing Lyme borreliosis, the investigators pointed to drawbacks in each method. Numerous false positive and false negative results have tended to compromise the reliability of serological testing. Positive results from cultivation have seldom been reported in the scientific literature.

On the premise that knowledge about *Bb in vitro* might lead to better understanding of the Lyme spirochetes *in vivo*, and this in turn might lead to more frequent detection of *Bb* when neuroborreliosis was suspected, Brorson et al examined structural alterations of *Bb* during exposure to spinal fluid.

Normal mobile spirochetes were inoculated into spinal fluid, where they converted to spheroplast L-forms after 1 to 24 hours. These cystic forms were transferred to a rich culture medium (BSK-H), where they converted to normal, mobile spirochetes after incubation for 9 to 17 days. The cultures were observed by darkfield microscopy, interference contrast microscopy, and transmission electron microscopy.

Included among the findings: After 24 hours of incubation, no normal spirochetes could be seen. All had transformed into cysts; the formation of cysts was somewhat different, however, depending on the concentration of protein in the spinal fluid. The cysts appeared to resemble the spheroplast L-forms seen by other researchers, which have defects in their cell wall manifested by resistance to á-lactam antibiotics.

As to what may occur *in vivo*: Brorson et al raised the possibility that normal spirochetes may often rapidly convert to cystic forms in spinal fluid, and routine microscopy would not recognize the altered *Bb* spirochetes. Thus, examination of the centrifuged spinal fluid by light or electron microscopy was important to achieve an accurate diagnosis and provide effective treatment, thereby stemming the disease and preventing irreversible neuronal damage.

Brorson (1998, 2)

Brorson et al published a second paper in *Infection* in 1998. Advancing their research on cystic forms of *Bb*, they reported on a rapid method of generating these forms. At the time of publication, the process for converting normal spirochetes into cysts and "re-transforming" the cysts into mobile spirochetes was both difficult and time consuming. Brorson et al had devised a quick method, which they hoped would facilitate examination of cystic forms in connection with conditions necessary for conversion, "products" detectable through PCR, resistance to antibiotics, and antigenic variation.

The investigators transferred mobile *Bb* spirochetes to distilled water, observing the cultures by darkfield microscopy (DFM), interference contrast microscopy (ICM), and transmission electron microscopy (TEM). Exposure lasted 4 hours. After 1 minute, 95% of the *Borrelia* had changed into cystic forms; after the full 4 minutes, no normal spirochetes were observed.

Transferring the cysts to BSK-II growth medium, the investigators again examined them microscopically. The cysts became smaller and more irregular, filling with organic substances. After 1 day, 1 to 5 "thin structures" sprouted from the cysts. These grew in length and thickness into "new-born spirochetes, at which time they detached from the cysts and showed normal mobility.

In their discussion, Brorson et al ventured the following from the *in vitro* results: "Similar cystic forms may occur in the human organism, and they may explain the long periods of latency, resistance to antibiotics, negative serological results, and low PCR sensitivity. For these reasons it is important to examine the antigens of the envelope of the cysts, DNA sequences for PCR analysis, and the cysts' sensitivity to antibiotics and other chemicals. It may be hypothesized that antigenic variation in *B. burgdorferi* occurs inside the cyst while the microbe is protected against external stress, and therefore antigens detected on the cyst envelope in vitro differ from the ones present in vivo...We believe the present method for rapid and easy generation of stable cysts will be a useful tool in further research."

Alban (2000)

Further research on atypical forms of *Bb* appeared in *Microbiology* in 2000. This paper, whose lead author was Dr. P. Scott Alban, reported on changes in *Bb* protein synthesis and structure induced by serum starvation.

Alban et al knew that Lyme spirochetes, incubated in BSK-II medium lacking rabbit serum, transform into non-motile cysts. (BSK-II ordinarily contains 6% rabbit serum and other meta-bolites.) They knew, too, that *Bb*, unlike most bacteria, cannot synthesize fatty acids *de novo*. Not supplementing the medium with animal serum, which provides fatty acids for growth *in vitro*, would "starve" *Bb*. (Not known at the time by the investigators was how *Bb* survives *in vivo* during tick molts and between tick blood meals–periods of starvation.)

The objectives of this study were to determine whether *Bb* cysts do, indeed, form as a result of a starvation-induced program (one which involves differential protein synthesis), the kinetics of cyst formation, and the viability of the encysted forms.

Depriving the *Bb* spirochetes of serum in a defined RPMI medium (which lacks serum but contains glucose, vitamins, and all 20 protein amino acids), the investigators noted that the cells became non-motile within a few hours. Within 48 hours, 90% of the vegetative spirochetes had changed into spherical cysts. When the researchers added tetracycline, they found that the antibiotic inhibited cyst formation, demonstrating that cyst formation required protein synthesis, that the cysts were not just degenerative forms. Adding either BSK-II or rabbit serum induced the cysts to open. The percentage of viable (vegetative) cells recovered from the opened cysts ranged from 2.9% to 52.5%, with viability inversely proportional to cyst age. Observations during the serum starvation and recovery investigations were made by phase-contrast microscopy and electron microscopy.

To examine protein synthesis by *Bb* during serum starvation, Alban et al labeled the cells with Trans35S-Label and analyzed the labeled cells by fluorography and 2-dimensional gel electrophoresis. Examination revealed the induced synthesis of over 20 proteins. To determine if any of these cyst proteins were antigenic, the investigators probed the cysts with sera from either *Bb*-infected humans or monkeys. They also tested proteins from vegetative cells with Western blots. The tests showed that several cyst proteins were antigenic.

These findings suggested that *Bb*, though possessing a small genome with limited biosynthesizing ability, rapidly responded to serum starvation by inducing changes in protein synthesis and cell shape–explaining how *Bb* survives nutrient deprivation in different hosts and host tissues and, conceivably, how it evades detection by the immune system.

ADDITIONAL READING

Radolf, JD et al, Analysis of *Borellia burgdorferi* membrane architecture by freeze-fracture electron microscopy, *Journal of Bacteriology*, 176;1994:21-31.

This paper, whose lead author was Dr. Justin D. Radolf, reported on an analysis of *Bb* by freeze-fracture electron microscopy. (This technique can visualize integral membrane proteins, thereby supplying information about the protein content and ultrastructure of biological membranes. It had been utilized to examine pathogenic and nonpathogenic spirochetes; there was, however, only a small amount of freeze-fracture data then available about the Lyme spirochete.)

By developing a more complete understanding of *Bb* membrane architecture, the investigators aimed to gain insights into the "potential" relationship of that architecture to the pathogenesis of Lyme disease, most critically the ways that Lyme spirochetes appear to evade host immune mechanisms.

The "hosts" in this study were mice and rabbits. The mice were inoculated with the "high-passage" (avirulent) B31 strain of *Bb* or high- and "low-passage" (virulent) isolates of the N40 *Bb* strain. The rabbits were inoculated with syphilis spirochetes.

A careful reading of the materials and methods section of this report is necessary to appreciate the findings, since the mass of technical detail prevents a simple summary. The abstract of the study gives a relatively large number of observations, which again are too densely technical for a simple summary explanation.

Re: the rabbits inoculated with syphilis–comparison of freeze-fractured *B. burgdorferi* and the syphilis spirochete revealed that the outer membrane architectures of these two pathogens differed markedly. The concluding sentence of the abstract, paraphrased here, conveys the clinical import of the study: The expression of poorly immunogenic, surface-exposed proteins as determinants of virulence may be part of the parasitic strategy used by *B. burgdorferi* to establish and maintain chronic infection in Lyme disease.

ANTIBIOTIC TREATMENT FOR PERSISTENT LYME DISEASE

Promptly diagnosed and treated with appropriate antibiotics, most cases of Lyme disease never progress beyond the early stage. But as the section in this update on diagnostic dilemmas illustrates, diagnosing Lyme borreliosis can be a complicated, uncertain process. The precise percentage of patients who relapse or develop chronic manifestations months and years after infection is hard to estimate, and experts vary in the percentages they venture. The scientific evidence presented in this section indicates, however, that a substantial number of patients with confirmed late Lyme require retreatment or repeated courses of antibiotic therapy, often over lengthy periods of time.

Note: papers published from the mid-1990s to 2003 are offered here in digest form. Papers published for the most part prior to the mid-1990s are offered as recommended reading. Note too: in papers appearing in European journals, when European patients are involved, the manifestations tend to be more neurotropic than those of US cases, because European and US strains of Lyme *Borrelia* are biologically different and can react differently to antibiotics.

PAPERS ON ANTIBIOTIC THERAPY FOR PERSISTENT

LYME DISEASE DIGESTED IN THIS SECTION

Asch, ES, et al, Lyme disease: an infectious and postinfectious syndrome, *The Journal of Rheumatology*, 1994; 21 (3): 454-60.

Valesov, M, et al, Long-term results in patients with Lyme arthritis following treatment with ceftriaxone, *Infection*, 1996; 24(1): 98-102.

Donta, ST, Tetracycline therapy or chronic Lyme disease, *Chronic Infectious Diseases*, 1997; 25 (Suppl 1):552-56.

Oksi, J, et al, Comparison of oral cefixime and intravenous ceftriaxone followed by oral amoxicillin in disseminated

Lyme borreliosis, *European Journal of the Clinical Microbiology of Infectious Diseases*, 1998; 17:715-19.

Oksi, J, et al, *Borrelia burgdorferi* detected by culture and PCR in clinical relapse of disseminated Lyme borreliosis, *Annals of Medicine*, 1999; 31:225-32.

Fallon, BA, et al, Repeated antibiotic treatment in chronic Lyme disease, *Journal of Spirochetal and Tick-borne Diseases*, 1999; 6 (Fall/Winter):94-101.

Fried MD et al, *Borrelia burgdorferi* persists in the gastrointestinal tract of children and adolescents with Lyme disease, *Journal of Spirochetal and Tick-borne Diseases,* Spring/Summer 2002; 9:11-15.

Krupp, LB, et al, Study and treatment of post Lyme disease: a randomized double masked clinical trial, *Neurology*, 2003: June 24;60(12:1923-30).

DIGESTS

Asch (1994)

The first paper digested here, appearing in *The Journal of Rheumatology* in 1994, reported on a systematic analysis of a large cohort of patients clinically diagnosed with Lyme disease. The primary aim was to establish the frequency and nature of acute and chronic morbidity. The investigators, Asch et al, retroactively evaluated 215 patients from an endemic Lyme area in the northeastern US. All fit the CDC case definition for Lyme, were diagnosed and treated with antibiotics at least a year prior to this evaluation, and were anti-*Borrelia* antibody positive.

The results showed relapses in 28% of the patients, reinfection in 18%, active disease in 9%, and persistence of symptoms in 53%. In summarizing these results, the authors stated that their study demonstrated that "despite recognition and antibiotic treatment of Lyme disease, significant infectious and postinfectious *sequelae* are common."

Valesov (1996)

A study published in *Infection* in 1996, the second paper digested in this section on long-term treatment for Lyme, reported on the outcome of a 36-month follow-up of cases of late-stage Lyme arthritis after 2-weeks of ceftriaxone therapy.

The researchers, Valesov et al, enrolled 35 patients in an open-label, non-comparative, international multicenter trial. Ten men and 25 women comprised the initial trial population, their ages ranging from 22 to 82. Diagnoses were confirmed by direct and indirect microbiological methods in addition to clinical symptoms. Treatment was given parenterally (IV or IM), 2 g once daily.

At 36 months, 26 of 33 patients were assessed. Of these, 19 had responded, six had experienced a relapse, and one presented a new manifestation. Before their consideration of possible mechanisms that might account for the significant percentage of relapsing cases, Valesov et al acknowledged that "the reasons for persistent symptoms in some Lyme arthritis patients still need to be explained."

Donta (1997)

Donta's report on tetracycline treatment for chronic Lyme, appearing in *Clinical Infectious Diseases* in 1997, broadened the study of typical symptoms of later-stage illness to include fatigue plus musculoskeletal pains, neuropsychiatric dysfunctions, and paresthesias. Between 1988 and 1995, he observed 277 patients who qualified for inclusion by having a combination of at least two of three sets of major manifestations. These patients received tetracycline for one to 11 months (mean=four months).

In 80% to 90% of the cases, Donta found that a three- to six-month course of therapy was associated with cure or significant improvement. Improvement showed as early as one to two weeks after the start of treatment; however, in patients with manifestations longer than a year, it frequently took four to six weeks on the antibiotic for evidence of any improvement. This slow rate of improvement, Donta speculated, "may correlate best with organisms for which the rates of multiplication and metabolism are slow, as is known for *B. burgdorferi*."

Noteworthy in Donta's discussion were several observations: The results of his study, he believed, supported the hypothesis that Lyme infection may be a persistent intracellular infection. (He referred to other chronic infections, which are known to have an intracellular reservoir.) The optimal criteria and methods for diagnosing and treating late-stage Lyme remain to be determined.

Oksi (1998)

The fourth digest here, a paper by Oksi et al published in 1998 in the *European Journal of Clinical Microbiology and Infectious Diseases*, reported on a randomized trial that compared cefexime to ceftriaxone. The former was taken orally for 100 days, combined with probenecid. The latter was given IV for 14 days, followed by oral amoxycillin in combination with probenecid for 100 days.

Two groups of 30 patients each participated, both groups diagnosed with disseminated Lyme borreliosis based on CDC clinical guidelines and lab findings. The mean age of the patients in the two groups was roughly the same (42+ years). All had been symptomatic for more than two months prior to diagnosis and beginning therapy for disseminated Lyme, and all were followed for a year after the start of antibiotic treatment.

Oksi et al found no statistically significant difference in outcome of infection between the groups, but in the cefixime group, both the total number of patients who relapsed or failed to respond and the number of post-therapy positive PCR findings were greater. Since 90% of the patients with disseminated infection had good responses to 3-4 months of therapy, the authors suggested that "prolonged courses of antibiotics may be beneficial in this setting."

Oksi (1999)

Another study on disseminated Lyme disease by Oksi et al–the fifth paper digested in this section–appeared in *Annals of Medicine* in 1999. This report followed 165 patients diagnosed between 1990 and 1994, all except one seropositive, and all previously treated with antibiotics. Its focus, though, was 13 patients who had clinical relapses and positive PCR cultures. These 13 patients had taken antibiotics for over three months, experiencing only temporary relief of symptoms.

Treated again for four to six weeks, usually with IV ceftriaxone, none of the patients was PCR positive afterward, and nine showed good therapeutic responses. In their discussion, Oksi et al considered "these 13 cases to have true treatment failure and not 'post-Lyme syndrome,'" noting that this observation supported earlier reports of Lyme patients with culture or PCR-proven treatment failures. They concluded that treating Lyme disease with appropriate antibiotics for "even more than three months" may not always eliminate *Bb* and suggested that "patients who do not respond favorably to the initial therapy should be followed up and repeatedly tested by PCR and culture and retreated if any of these testes is positive when several months have elapsed since the first treatment."

Fallon (1999)

A report by Fallon et al on repeated antibiotic treatment in chronic Lyme disease, published in the *Journal of Spirochetal and Tickborne Diseases* in 1999, is the last digest here. Fallon et al enrolled 23 Lyme patients who complained of persistent memory difficulties after IV antibiotic therapy of four to 16 weeks. These patients were evaluated at baseline and reevaluated four months later. Between baseline and reevaluation, 18 of the 23 patients received additional antibiotics.

At the baseline, for those subjects later given antibiotics and those subjects not treated, there was no statistically significant difference between the groups in anxiety, cognition, or depression. At reevaluation, patients given IV antibiotics scored better on cognition tests than untreated patients. The former also showed the greatest functional improvement in energy, pain, physical functioning. The results of their uncontrolled pilot study suggested to the researchers that repeated courses of antibiotics may result in objectively measurable improvement in cognition after a four-month interval in patients previously receiving more than the standard recommended antibiotic treatment.

Further, suggested Fallon et al, the results of their small study in the *Journal of Spirochetal and Tick-borne Diseases* were "consistent with the observations of physicians who note that many patients with persistent symptoms appear to benefit from repeated courses of antibiotic therapy, a phenomenon supportive of the persistent infection hypothesis." They urged testing of their suggestive findings in a blinded, placebo-controlled, randomized trial enrolling a much larger number of chronic Lyme patients.

Fried (2002)

Fried and his co-investigators reported on a study that documented the persistence of *B. burgdorferi* DNA in the gastrointestinal (GI) tract of children with Lyme disease who had been treated with antibiotics. Five boys and five girls, ranging from 9 to 13 years in age, were evaluated consecutively. They manifested chronic abdominal pain, heartburn, or bright red blood in the stool that had persisted for at least a year after onset of an EM rash. Western blots showed positive for Lyme. In all cases, antibiotic therapy for Lyme had been started within one year of the EM rash and initial Lyme symptoms.

The researchers examined GI biopsies for *Bb*, using a Dieterle stain, and with PCR to OspA of *Bb*. They used endoscopy to assess the GI mucosa for inflammation. Ten consecutive children used as controls were also tested by the same means.

In the Lyme patients, examination revealed chronic colitis, chronic duodenitis, and chronic gastritis. These conditions appeared associated with detection of *Bb* DNA in the GI tract despite previous antibiotic therapy. None of the biopsies of the control subjects were PCR positive for *Bb*.

Discussing the results, Fried et al remarked: "Several... authors have suggested that *B. burgdorferi* may persist in humans and animals for months or years, despite strong humoral or immune responses. One possible explanation for this persistence is the failure of the host to produce *Borreliacidal* OspA antibodies. Another possible explanation is the invasion of poorly vascularized connective tissue by spirochetes or even an intracellular location of spirochetes."

The investigators advised: "other etiologic infections that are also transmitted by a tick bite should be considered in the differential diagnosis of heartburn, abdominal pain, and blood in the stool in Lyme disease patients with persistent symptoms. Coinfection with either Babesia, Ehrlichia, and Bartonella have recently been reported."

Krupp (2003)

In 2001, Klempner et al had published a report in *The New England Journal of Medicine* on two randomized trials involving patients whose symptoms persisted after the recommended antibiotic treatment for acute Lyme (*New Engl J Med*, 2001; Vol. 345, Issue 2: 85-92). One group consisted of 78 patients, sero-positive for IgG antibodies at enrollment. The other group comprised 51 seronegative patients. All had complained of chronic symptoms and had a well-documented history of antibiotic treatment. Patients were randomly given either IV ceftriaxone, followed by oral doxycycline for 8 weeks, or matching IV and placebo. Using the SF-36, a self-report scale of functional ability, as the primary outcome measure, Klempner et al found no difference between the groups in degree of improvement based on treatment. (For further discussion of Klempner, see the Policy section of the *Lyme Disease Update*, under the subhead "National Institutes of Health.")

Krupp et al reported in *Neurology* in 2003 on a randomized double-blinded clinical trial in 55 patients with well-documented chronic Lyme and previous antibiotic therapy who met a pre-determined level of severe fatigue. Using the Fatigue Severity Scale as the primary outcome measure, these investigators randomly assigned patients either IV ceftriaxone or matching placebo for 4 weeks. At 6 months, on the primary measure of outcome, Krupp et al found that 64% of patients given antibiotics were improved compared with 18.5% given placebo. Further, for patients with positive Western blots at baseline, on the fatigue measure, the antibiotic vs. placebo responder rate was 80% vs. 13%. For seronegative patients, the responder rate was 46% vs. 27%. Patients receiving antibiotics also had significantly lower pain scores than those receiving placebo.

Neither Klempner nor Krupp observed improved cognition on neuro-psychological tests, but the majority of patients recruited for both studies didn't manifest significant cognitive impairment on enrollment. Note: Klempner et al in 2001 and Krupp et al in 2003 offered contradictory findings: Krupp indicating that repeated antibiotic therapy had a substantial positive effect, Klempner indicating no effect. Methodological factors, though, could have contributed to the conflicting findings. Different primary outcome measures were employed, SF-36 in Klempner, Fatigue Severity Scale in Krupp. The relative homogeneity of the sample may have played a part (patients with mixed symptom profiles in Klempner, only patients with a pre-determined severity level of fatigue in Krupp).

ADDITIONAL READING

Berger, BW, Treating erythema chronicum migrans of Lyme disease, *Journal of the American Academy of Dermatology*, 1986;15:459-63

Berger evaluated 117 patients (102 adults and 15 children), diagnosed with EM between 6/81 and 9/85. The evaluation was undertaken to prevent the late manifestations of Lyme and reduce the need for retreatment. Of the total patient group, 56 with mild illness didn't progress to later-stage signs and symptoms or require follow-up antibiotics.

Out of 61 patients with a major form of Lyme infection, 14 required retreatment. Five developed post-treatment signs of Bell's palsy and chronic joint pain. Berger assessed the effectiveness of a handful of different antibiotics, finding tetracycline and penicillin the most effective, especially with probenecid added in cases with acute forms of Lyme.

Schoen, RT, Treatment of Lyme disease, *Connecticut Medicine*, 1989;53(No.6):335-37. Schoen reviewed what was known by the late 1980s about treatment for early and late stages of Lyme borreliosis. The goals of antibiotic therapy in the early stage, he remarked, were to shorten the duration of infection and prevent progression of *Bb* infection to late disease. Later Lyme, he noted, proved frequently harder to treat, necessitating prolonged oral or IV antibiotic therapy.

At that time, the recommended antibiotics for early Lyme were oral tetracycline or doxycycline, with the dosage and length of treatment dependent on the severity of infection. "The greatest challenge in the treatment of early Lyme disease," Schoen declared, "is the recognition of this infection in a diverse group of patients, not all of whom have EM, and many of whom have mild or nonspecific constitutional symptoms. Serologic testing provides only limited help in identifying individuals with early Lyme disease."

Concerning later-stage illness, he cautioned that "not all patients with neurologic manifestations or with arthritis respond to oral or intravenous antibiotic therapy." He advised that "in many of these individuals, retreatment may be necessary."

Steere, A, Medical progress: Lyme disease, *The New England Journal of Medicine*, 1989; 321 (No. 9):586-96

Steere's paper on Lyme reviewed studies in print on the cause, vector, epidemiology, clinical signs, pathogenesis, diagnosis, and treatment of "this protean infection" (Steere's words). Steere's report on a cluster of arthritis cases in CT in 1977 had been instrumental in establishing Lyme disease as a separate entity.

What Steere had to say about Lyme treatment in the late 1980s is now mainly of historical interest. Two of his findings about antibiotic therapy stand out. (1) A randomized study had indicated that tetracycline was more effective than penicillin V and erythromycin for early Lyme. High-dose IV penicillin gave beneficial results for most neurological manifestations of later stage infection.

Steere's discussion of problems involving appropriate treatment raised several unresolved questions worth noting today. Should tick bites be treated with prophylactic antibiotic therapy? Should all pregnant women with Lyme disease be given high-dose IV penicillin? (A woman in Europe, treated for EM with oral antibiotics during pregnancy, gave birth to a baby who died of possible Lyme encephalitis, prompting some physicians to give high-dose IV antibiotics to all pregnant women.) The answers to these questions were unclear.

Summing up, Steere wrote: "Treatment with appropriate antibiotics is usually curative, but longer courses of therapy are often needed later in the illness, and some patients may not respond."

Hassler, D, et al, Pulsed high-dose cefotaxime therapy in refractory Lyme borreliosis, *The Lancet* (letter to the editor), Vol. 338: July 20, 1991

Reporting on two cases of Lyme infection resistant to treatment, Hassler et al noted that by 1991, controlled trials had demonstrated that third-generation cephalosporins had become the therapy of choice for late Lyme disease. One treatment cycle "cured" about 90% of patients.

On the presumption that *Bb* may lack sensitivity to antibiotics because of its long generation time (not all the microorganisms divide during treatment), Hassler et al tried pulsed high-dose cefotaxime in the two refractory cases they followed. The first patient received IV drips for two days, followed by six antibiotic-free days, with the cycle repeated six times. The second patient received three doses on the same day, followed by six drug-free days, over ten weeks. The first patient was still symptom-free six months after pulsed high-dose cefotaxime. Skin biopsies of the second patient after the pulsed high-dose treatment were negative.

(Skin biopsies after various previous antibiotic treatments, between 1988 and 1990, had repeatedly contained *Borrelia*.)

Hassler et al concluded that in certain Lyme cases, elimination of *Bb* may depend on proliferation of *Borreliae* during the treatment period, or on sufficient concentration of an antibiotic with good anti-*Bb* activity in all affected tissues.

Cimmino, MA, et al, Long term treatment of chronic Lyme arthritis with benzathine penicillin, *Annals Rheumatic Disease*, 1992;51:1007-08

This paper reported on two cases of chronic Lyme arthritis refractory to standard antibiotic treatment, which long-term benzathine penicillin cured. In their discussion of these cases, Cimmino et al offered a number of explanations for the lack of response to the recommended regimens, including: the persistence of spirochetes in intracellular locations, in certain organs, e.g., spleen, and in synovial membranes. The authors expressed the belief that long-term benzathine penicllin therapy may eliminate *Bb* through lysis of the spirochetes when they temporarily leave their sanctuaries or by inhibition of spirochete reproduction.

Preac-Mursic, V, et al, Kill kinetics of *Borrelia burgdorferi* and bacterial findings in relation to the treatment of Lyme borreliosis, *Infection*, 1996; Vol. 1, No. 1:9-16

In an attempt to arrive at a clearer understanding of why *Bb* persists after antibiotic therapy, Preac-Mursic et al determined the killing effects of amoxicillin, azithromycin, cefotaxime, ceftri-axone, doxycycline, and penicillin G. The results of their investigation showed that the killing rate of a given antibiotic appeared more dependent on the reaction time than on the concentration of the antibiotic. Also noted among the findings: The *B. afzelii* and *B. garinii* strains of the Lyme spirochete (predominant in Asia and Europe, respectively) react differently to antibiotics; and different reactions to a given antibiotic exist within one species.

Discussing their evaluation, the authors pointed out that "the reason for the persistence of *B. burgdorferi s.l.* in patients after treatment with antibiotics is not completely understood." They then elaborated: "In fact a number of factors may play a role, e.g. virulence of *Borreliae*, long generation time of *Borreliae*, biologic differences in strains, the site of the infection, insufficient antibiotic therapy and many others. To what extent the immunological status of a patient is of importance is unknown. The capacity of *Borrelia burgdorferi* to hide in various human tissues (heart, muscle, spleen, eyes, brain), intracellular localization and an insufficient antibiotic tissue level are critical for the therapy."

Cimmino, MA, et al, Treatment of Lyme arthritis, *Infection*, 1996; Vol. 1, No. 1:91-94

Here, in 1996, Cimmino et al reviewed evaluations of various antibiotic treatments that had appeared in peer-review journals between 1985 and 1991. Almost all these published studies were small or medium-sized and not blinded. The antibiotics included (in adults): benzathine penicillin, IV penicillin G, IV ceftriaxone, IV cefotaxime, and oral doxycycline or amoxicillin plus pro-benecid. Concluding, the authors stated: "There is no consensus on the therapeutic protocol to be adopted in Lyme arthritis. Many questions are still open about the antibiotic agents to adopt as well as the best duration of treatment."

Luft, BJ, et al, Azithromycin compared with amoxicillin in the treatment of erythema migrans, *Annals of Internal Medicine*, 1996;124:785-91

The purpose of this randomized, double-blind, double-dummy, multicenter study which started with 246 patients with EM was to compare azithromycin with amoxicillin in resolving the characteristic early-stage rash and preventing later stage Lyme disease. Eventually, 217 patients proved evaluable. The results indicated that a 20-day course of amoxicillin was more effective than azithromycin for EM. Among the other findings: Patients given azithromycin experienced a greater relapse rate (16%) than those on amoxycillin (4%). Most patients were seronegative on

Lyme ELISAs at the time of presentation with EM (65%), and also at the time of relapse (57%).

Luft et al concluded: "This prospective study confirmed our previous observation that a subpopulation of patients treated promptly but ineffectively for erythema migrans may ultimately develop later manifestations of Lyme disease and be seronegative on ELISA tests for *B. burgdorferi* at the time of relapse. The finding that patients can have relapse and be seronegative indicates that serologic assays are not reliable in the assessment of patients who have been treated for early Lyme disease. Great care must be taken to document all objective abnormalities in these patients. With the advent of new technologies such as Western blotting analysis, polymerase chain reaction, and antigen capture, these assays will be increasingly important in defining this difficult patient population."

Brouqui, P, et al, Eucaryotic cells protect *Borrelia burgdorferi* from the action of penicillin and ceftriaxone but not from the action of doxycycline and erythromycin, *Antimicrobial Agents and Chemotherapy*, June. 1996; pp. 1552-54

Based on observations of relapses after appropriate therapy for Lyme disease, and on studies suggesting that *Bb* might "dissimulate within certain host cells and therefore escape immune response and the actions of antibiotics" (as this report put it), Brouqui et al hypothesized that only antibiotics with good intracellular distribution would definitively eradicate the Lyme spirochetes. Evaluating regimens of ceftriaxone, doxycycline, erythromycin, and penicillin, the researchers determined that when *Bb* was grown in the presence of eucaryotic cells, these cells had a protective effect against ceftriaxone and penicillin, an effect which did not develop with the administration of doxycycline and erythromycin.

TICK-BORNE DISEASES ASSOCIATED WITH LYME BORRELIOSIS

The ticks serving as vectors for Lyme disease also transmit other microorganisms that can infect humans. Babesiosis, ehrlichiosis, Rocky Mountain spotted fever, and bartonella are the main co-infections. This fifth evidence section of the LDA update on Lyme borreliosis supplies basic information about the cause, transmission, incidence, manifestations, diagnosis, confirming lab tests, and treatment of these associated tick-borne conditions.

Many physicians are relatively unacquainted with the signs and symptoms of the tick-borne conditions associated with Lyme, so an unknown number of people in the US may go untreated for such infections, especially since they can pass asymptomatically.

Patients who have Lyme disease together with a co-infection may remain mysteriously ill and unresponsive to standard treatment. The information offered here may explain some of these treatment failures and help guide physicians in recognizing the concurrent diseases. This section closes with articles recommended for further reading.

BABESIOSIS

Cause

Two species of intraerythrocytic protozoal parasites, belonging to the more than 100 species of babesia, are the pathogens responsible for most babesiosis infections in humans: *Babesia microti* in North America, and *Babesia divergens* in Europe.[1,2] *B. microti* also infects various primates and small mammals. Cattle are the main animal host of *B. divergens*, but recently this species of *Babesia* has been found in rats and gerbils.[2] WA1, apparently a new species of *Babesia*, has been identified in humans in California, Georgia, and Washington.[1]

---

[1] *Current medical diagnosis & treatment*, Lang Medical Books-McGraw Hill (39th ed., NY, 2000).

Transmission

The vector for babesiosis is the *Ixodes* tick, the same arthropod vector for Lyme disease, particularly *Ixodes scapularis* and *Ixodes ricinus*.[2] There are reports of transmission, however, from blood transfusion as well.[1,2] The chief animal hosts for babesiosis in the US are the white-footed mouse and white-tailed deer, also the preferred animal hosts for the Lyme disease spirochete. The *Babesia* protozoa enter the tick while it feeds off the animal host, multiply in the gut wall of the tick, and spread to the tick's salivary glands.[2] When the tick bites a human, the *Babesia* parasites invade the red blood cells and multiply, resulting in rupture of these cells, and leading to invasion of other red blood cells.[1]

Incidence

In the past, human babesiosis infections have been occasionally reported outside the US, but now case reports are increasing abroad[1,2] In the US, several hundred *B. microti* infections have been reported in mid-Atlantic and northeastern states, mostly from coastal and island regions. Reports of babesiosis have come from other states, including California, Minnesota, Missouri, Washington, and Wisconsin.[1] But the most endemic areas in the US are Connecticut and islands along the Massachusetts and New York coasts, especially eastern and south central Long Island, NY.[2] A reliable estimate of the incidence of babesiosis in the US is hard to make because infections frequently are asymptomatic and overall surveillance of cases is limited. (One estimate, for instance, says that 10% of patients with Lyme in southern New England also suffer from babesiosis in places where–under natural conditions– both diseases are transmissible from animals to humans. This estimate adds that babesiosis may be relatively common as well in endemic regions of states in the northeast and upper midwest.)[2]

---

[2] Mylonakis, M, When to suspect and how to monitor babesiosis, *American Family Physician*, 2001;62 (No. 10).

Signs & Symptoms

After a tick bite, the incubation period ranges from five to 33 days. After a blood transfusion, it may last up to nine weeks. Most patients, however, do not recall a bite. People of all ages may contract babesiosis,[1,3] manifestations of which often overlap the manifestations of Lyme borreliosis. As noted above, subclinical infections are common.[1,3]

Early signs and symptoms of babesiosis infection include weakness, irregular high fever, headache, fatigue, diaphoresis, day and night sweats, chills, and anorexia. Note: Not characteristic of this disease is the periodicity of signs and symptoms found in malaria, another protozoal parasitic illness,[1,2,3] and rash is an uncommon early clinical sign. Physical examination may show evidence of shock, hepatomegaly, and splenomegaly. Clinical signs of CNS involvement include altered emotional and sensorium lability, back and neck stiffness, headache, and photophobia. Patients may pass dark urine and develop jaundice if babesiosis progresses to a later stage.[2]

The most frequent complications of babesiosis are acute respiratory distress syndrome, congestive heart failure, disseminated intravascular coagulation, and elevated BUN and creatine readings. Acute respiratory distress may occur a few days after the beginning of antimicrobial therapy. Heart attack and kidney failure have also been reported in patients severely ill with babesiosis.[2,3]

Diagnosis

Common nonspecific findings in babesiosis are a slightly depressed leukocyte count and mild to severe hemolytic anemia.[2] In conjunction with epidemiological information, a Wright– or Giemsa-stained blood smear is usually ordered for lab confirmation, and repeated smears may be required. Parasitemia normally shows in 2-4 weeks, and smears are often negative in

---

[3] Horowitz, RI, Treatment roundtable: different approaches to chronic Lyme disease, paper delivered at the 12th International Scientific Conference on Lyme Disease, NYC, April 1999.

patients not having a high level of parasitemia–over 5%. Because the *babesia* microorganisms resemble malarial parasites (particularly *Plasmodium falciparum*), it is crucial in testing to distinguish between the two pathogens. *Babesial* protozoa normally form tetrads and don't show iron-bearing pigments and extracellular merozoites.[1,2,3]

Serum antibody presence by IFA (indirect immunofluorescent assay) appears within 2-4 weeks, and may persist for half a year to a year. Cross reactions between *babesial* and malarial parasitic species are possible; if this cross reaction occurs, the infecting microorganism as a rule produces the highest antibody titers. An additional complicating factor in IFA testing is that different labs use different protocols to determine a positive result, so determinations can vary accordingly.[1,2]

Detection of *B. microti* by polymerase chain reaction (PCR) tends to be equally specific but more sensitive than IFA in diagnosing acute babesiosis.[1,2] Serial PCR analyses (at least five consecutive specimens), have helped confirm babesiosis in seronegative cases.[3]

Treatment

Quinine in combination with clindamycin for seven to ten days used to be the antibabesial therapy of choice. Other drugs have been evaluated, with varying results.[1,2] Recent reports indicate that azithromycin plus either quinine or atovaquone suspension may also be effective.[1]

In closing this subsection of information about babesiosis, the following findings should be noted: The end result of babesiosis infection in humans seems to be influenced by cell-mediated and humoral immune mechanisms. States of immunodeficiency, previous removal of the spleen, and advanced age may factor into the development of severe illness.[2]

In extremely ill patients (with asplenia, massive hemolysis, and blood parasitemia over 10%), treatment with antibabesial chemotherapeutic agents in combination with exchange blood transfusions may be necessary.[2]

Despite extensive antibiotic therapy, babesiosis has been shown to persist in humans. Although babesiosis tends to be self-limited in most cases, untreated silent infection may linger for many months.[1,2,3]

Persistence of circulating *Babesia* DNA for three or more months in people who are asymptomatic and untreated, demonstrated in a recent study, raises the question of whether treatment is appropriate regardless of symptoms.[1]

EHRLICHIOSIS

Cause

Three tick-borne species of bacteria belonging to the *Ehrlichia* genus have been recognized since the mid-1980s as causing human infection in the US: *Ehrlichia chaffeensis*, *E. ewingii*, and *E. phagocytophila*. (One species, *E. sennetsu*, recognized in Japan since 1953, appears to be the only other known cause of human ehrlichiosis, and this species is rare outside S.E. Asia and the Far East.)[4]

Ehrlichia are gram-negative, nonmotile, rickettsial bacteria. As intracellular parasites, they infect the cytoplasm of reticuloendothelial cells and circulating leukocytes.[5] They multiply as phagosomes in microscopic colonies, forming characteristic inclusions observable with Giemsa's stain.[1]

E. Chaffeensis causes human monocytic ehrlichiosis (HME). Human granulytic ehrlichiosis (HGE), the second *Ehrlichian* infection recognized in the US, is caused by a pathogen not yet formally named. The CDC, though, recently changed the name of HGE to *Anaplasma Phagocytophila*. Described first in 1994, this species seems closely related or perhaps identical to the veterinary species *E. phagocytophila* and *E. Equi*.[4] The third, and latest,

---

[4] Viral and Rickettsial Zoonoses Branch, Human ehrlichiosis in the US, Center for Disease Control; web page (reviewed 4/5/2000) @ http://www.cdc.gov/ncidod/dvrd/ehrlichia/Index.htm

[5] *Miriam-Webster's Medical Dictionary*, Miriam-Webster, Inc. (Springfield, MA, 1995).

Ehrlichian infection to be recognized, *E. ewingii*, so far appears to be limited to a comparatively small number of patients with underlying immunosuppression in MO, OK, and TN.[4]

Transmission

The lone star tick (*Amblyomma americanum*) is the vector for HME. For HGE, the primary vectors are the ticks that transmit Lyme (*Ixodes scapularis*, and *Ixodes pacificus* in the western US). Vectors for *E. ewingii* infection have not been fully investigated.[1,4]

Incidence

Reports of HME have originated chiefly in the southeastern, south central, and mid-Atlantic regions of the US. While the full geographic boundaries of HGE are still being "mapped," HGE and Lyme appear to extend over similar portions of the country. The geographic range and vectors for *E. ewingii* infections remain uncertain.[1,4] The incidence of HGE is highest in summer, but in warm areas of the US, there are year-round reports of cases.[1]

Signs & Symptoms

HME and HGE manifest similarly. After a roughly nine-day incubation period, patients develop a febrile illness, acute at the onset, and they experience some combination of the following manifestations: arthralgia, chills, gastrointestinal trouble, headache, malaise, myalgia, nausea, and rigors. A pleomorphic rash is common in HME, but uncommon in HGE. If ehrlichiosis persists, the fever and headache worsen.

If not treated or not treated promptly, HGE may have serious complications, including: acute renal failure, acute respiratory failure, disseminated intravascular coagulation, encephalopathy, and meningitis.[1,2,3,6] Note: Delay or failure to treat HGE has been associated with death.[6]

---

[6] Babesiosis, ehrlichiosis: Lyme disease coinfections on the rise, can complicate treatment, *Family Practice News*, 2002; 32 (No. 19).

Diagnosis

The diagnosis of ehrlichiosis is based on a history of tick exposure, evaluation of clinical signs to determine if they are characteristic, and lab tests for confirmation. IFA is available, requiring both acute and convalescent sera, and PCR assays of whole blood samples may speed confirmation of a diagnosis.[1] Both HME and HGE may have similar abnormal lab findings: elevated liver enzymes (ALT and AST), intracytoplasmic colonies in leukocytes (on a bone aspirate, biopsy, cerebrospinal fluid, or peripheral smear), leukopenia, lymphopenia, and thrombocytopenia.[3]

Treatment

The current preferred antibiotic therapy for HME and HGE, when ehrlichiosis is the only tick-borne infection involved, is oral or IV doxycycline for five to seven days or until the patient is fever-free for three days.[4,6]

ROCKY MOUNTAIN SPOTTED FEVER

Cause

A bacterium of the genus *Rickettsia* (*R. ricketsii*) is the pathogen responsible for Rocky Mountain spotted fever (RMSF).[5]

Transmission

Several different arthropod vectors transmit this acute infection to humans: the wood tick (*Dermacentor andersoni*) in the western US, the dog tick (*Dermacentor variabilis*) in the eastern US, and the deer tick (*Ixodes)* that transmits Lyme borreliosis.[1]

Incidence

About a thousand cases are reported annually, mostly in the eastern third of the US. Late spring through summer is the peak time for infection.[1]

Signs & Symptoms

The first signs and symptoms of RMSF manifest 2-14 days after a tick bite and include chills, fever, headache, insomnia, irritability, myalgias, nausea, prostration, restlessness, and vomiting. These initial manifestations may be followed by coughing and pneumonitis. Coma, delirium, lethargy, seizures, and stupor may occasionally develop. Between the second and sixth day after the onset of fever, a reddish or purplish rash usually appears, first on the ankles and wrists, afterward spreading to the arms, legs, and trunk. In 10% of cases, the rash is minimal or doesn't develop. The initial faint macules progress to maculopapules, then petechiae. Characteristically, the rash involves the palms and soles. Complications in some patients include gangrene, hepatomegaly, jaundice, myocarditis, splenomegaly, and uremia.[1]

Note: Sequelae occur more often than previously realized in RMSF, including bladder and bowel incontinence, cerebellar and vestibular dysfunction, encephalopathy, loss of hearing, motor deficits, paraparesis, peripheral neuropathy, and seizures. In untreated children, the mortality rate for RMSF is under 20%. In untreated elderly people, the rate may reach 70%. The main cause of death is pneumonitis with cardiac or respiratory failure.[1]

Diagnosis

The early manifestations of RMSF resemble the symptoms and signs of numerous other diseases, e.g., the rash may look like the rashes in ehrlichiosis, measles, or typhoid. Thus, a differential diagnosis is imperative.

Complement fixation, IFA, or latex agglutination are tests that can be utilized to establish a diagnosis. None of these commercial tests, however, can confirm RMSF in its early clinical course, but in the second week after infection they can detect a rise in antibody titer.[1]

Abnormal lab findings include hematuria, hyponatremia, leukocytosis, proteinuria, and thrombocytopenia. A mild pleocytosis and hypoglycorrhachia may show in the CSF. Activation of platelets, coagulation pathways, and fibrin breakdown may also occur because of endothelial damage.[1]

Treatment

Where no other bacterial or protozoal infections are concurrent, RMSF is treated with oral or IV chloramphenicol or oral or IV doxycycline for seven days or through the third day without fever. This infection usually responds quickly to early antibiotic treatment.[1]

BARTONELLA

Cause

Bartonella infections are induced by gram negative, intracellular bacteria. The *Bartonella* genus includes *Bartonella henselae*, the form described here.

Transmission

Several vectors appear to transmit the various organisms of the *Bartonella* genus, ticks among them. A recently published small case series of patients in NJ reported that *B. henselae*-specific DNA had been detected in live deer ticks taken from the homes of two of these patients.[7]

Incidence

Prior to the study of NJ patients referred to above, published in 2001, there had been no reported cases of tick-borne *B. henselae* (*Bh*) infection in humans. Note: Knowledge about vector transmission of Bartonella organisms is incomplete,[7] so information about the incidence of *Bh* infection in human is still correspondingly sketchy.

---

[7] Eskow E et al, Concurrent infection of the central nervous system by *Borrelia burgdorferi* and *Bartonella henselae*, *Arch Neurol*, 2001;58:1357-1363.

Signs & Symptoms

Bh may invade the central nervous system, causing various neurological manifestations.[7] Cases of encephalopathy have been documented, where patients complain of generalized, persistent headache and restlessness. Some of these patients may suffer seizures, ranging from brief to status epilepticus, from focal to generalized. Dementia following encephalitis and loss of vision have also been documented. It is theorized that *B. henselae*-induced encephalopathy may often result in status epilepticus in school-age children.[7]

Diagnosis

In the NJ study above, all patients showed various levels of *Bh*-specific antibodies on IFA tests, but the authors cautioned that serologic tests alone have limited value in diagnosing *B. henselae* infection. The investigators also observed that the sensitivity of culture for this pathogen is low compared to PCR detection, the latter being useful in cases with a broad differential diagnosis.[7]

Treatment

Azithromycin has proven effective against *B. henselae*.[8] One patient in the NJ study seems to have improved after a 28-day course of cefotaxime therapy. Three other patients in this study had a history of chronic Lyme, with persistent manifestations despite previous antibiotic treatment, and the concurrent findings of both *Bb* and *B. henselae*-specific DNA in their CSF may account for the earlier lack of response to antibiotics given exclusively for Lyme.[7]

NOTE: AT PRESS TIME: Acording to Adelson M et al, "As treatment for *Bartonella* infections varies from that prescribed for LD patients, physicians should add *Bartonella* infections to the list of possible coinfection agents when evaluating patients in regions of

---

[8] Bass JW et al, Prospective randomized double-blind placebo-controlled evaluation of azithromycin for treatment of cat scratch disease, *Pediatr Infect Dis J* , 1998;17:447-452.

tick endemicity...Further studies need to clarify that the *Bartonella ssp.* can be passed in culturable form from vector to host and to identify which species of *Bartonella* are present. [8a]

ADDITIONAL READING

Horowitz, RI, Treatment roundtable: different approaches to chronic Lyme disease (paper delivered at the 12th International Scientific Conference on Lyme Disease, NYC, April 1999). In 1999, Dr. Horowitz was Assistant Director of Medicine, Vassar Brothers Hospital, Poughkeepsie, NY.

Mylonakis, M, When to suspect and how to monitor babesiosis, *American Family Physician*, Vol. 62, No. 10, 5/15/2001.

Babesiosis, ehrlichiosis: Lyme disease coinfections on the rise, can complicate treatment, *Family Practice News*, Vol. 32, No. 19, 10/1/2002.

Human ehrlichiosis in the US, Information put on the web site of the Center for Disease Control and Prevention, the Viral and Rickettsial Zoonoses Branch, web page reviewed 4/5/2000. This web page is accessible at http://www.cdc.gov/ncidod/dvrd/ehrlichia/Index.htm

Eskow E et al, Concurrent infection of the central nervous system by *Borrelia burgdorferi* and *Bartonella henselae*, *Arch Neurol*, 2001;58:1357-1363.

[8a] Adelson, M et al, Prevalence of *Borrelia burgdorferi, Bartonella* spp., *Babesia microti,* and *Anaplasma phagocytophila* in *Ixodes scapularis* Ticks Collected in Northern New Jersey, *Journal of Clinical Microbiology*, June 2004, p2799-2801.

POLICY SECTION

Lyme Disease Update:
Policy/Political Activism

This section of the *Lyme Disease Update* features political activities by Lyme disease patients and their families. Primarily, these affected individuals aim to initiate government programs and studies that not only improve chances for recovery and a resumption of normal life, but also stop the spread of Lyme disease.

A paragraph from a paper on neuropsychiatric Lyme borreliosis, published in the *Psychiatric Quarterly* in 1992, conveyed the medical concerns of such patients. A dozen years later, this depiction remains valid for patients with various complications of Lyme.

"Many patients have felt abandoned by their medical doctors when the diagnosis was uncertain and the treatment not fully curative. Others have had to see many different doctors before one was able to put together the diversity of their symptoms and come up with a diagnosis. Several patients have said that the hardest thing to bear–even more than the pain and disability–had been the feeling that they were somehow inexplicably altered, in their emotions and personality and ability to function, without hope of finding a cause or a cure, and without a doctor who could honor their difficulty, whether or not he or she could solve it. For some patients then, the ambiguities surrounding diagnosis and treatment and the consequent sense of abandonment by medical professionals were among the most distressing aspects of the illness experience."[1]

A quote from "Animal-borne Epidemics out of control: threatening the Nation's Health" (supported by grants from Pew Charitable Trust and Palmer Foundation) best expresses the reasons patients nationwide have taken political action:

> While cooperation now exists between the federal, state, and local departments and officials in charge of controlling the disease, Lyme disease has become a permanent part of America's public health landscape. It provides a warning and

---

[1] Fallon BA et al, The neuropsychiatric manifestations of Lyme borreliosis, *Psychiatric Quarterly*, Spring 1992; 63(1):96-117.

example of how an apparent state or regionally-centered problem can grow to become a national problem. Instead of implementing a proactive nationwide animal-borne disease management strategy, the public health response to Lyme disease was left to evolve as the disease spread across the country.[1a]

[1a] Trust for America's Health, issue report, August 2003
www.HealthyAmericans.org

HISTORY OF GROUP ACTIVITY BY LYME PATIENTS

Shortly after Lyme disease was described in the mid-1970s as a distinct pathological condition, patients in states where clusters of cases had been reported formed local groups to learn more about this illness. Identification of the Lyme spirochete in the early 1980s fostered the wider development of such groups.

Politically-related activity on behalf of patients began as an outgrowth of these local groups in the late 1980s. To date, organizations concerned about Lyme have convinced government officials in at least 16 states to gather and publish information about the diagnosis, spread, and treatment of Lyme disease and its associated infections.

Several of these organizations initiated political activity on the federal level of government in the early 1990s. Transformation of the Lyme Disease Association of NJ, Inc. into the Lyme Disease Association, Inc. (LDA) in 1999 has provided an umbrella organization under which state and other local organizations can coordinate their work on the national level.

In 2003, LDA was successful in obtaining a meeting with the office of the Secretary of Health & Human Services (HHS) in Washington, DC. LDA pulled together a national team including doctors, state officials, and activists. The team presented to HHS and to the top officials of the CDC and NIH who were video-teleconferenced into the meeting issues including the following: the problems created for patients and physicians by the misuse of the CDC surveillance criteria for diagnosis, the testing problems, the lack of funding for Lyme disease research, and the lack of public and physician education.

GOALS OF POLITICAL ACTIVITY BY LYME PATIENTS

Two factors drive the Lyme activists. (1) State by state, reports of Lyme cases and cases of associated tick-borne diseases are on the rise: Lyme is now the most prevalent vector-borne disease in the US. (2) Uncertainty over diagnosis and treatment continues. Referring to this situation at the turn of the millennium, a Texas legislative report on tick-borne diseases declared:

"The amount of useful information regarding the effective diagnosis and treatment of some tick-borne illnesses has been insufficient to foster a consensus within the scientific and medical communities."[2]

Presently, most experts do agree about what happens in the great majority of cases. When bitten by ticks transmitting Lyme disease, diagnosed early, and given adequate antibiotic therapy, patients generally have a less severe form of Lyme and less frequently develop long-term complications or recurrences.

A significant percentage of infected people, though, are not diagnosed at the onset of infection, and thus are not treated in time to avoid sequelae. These people and their families constitute the core of the Lyme action groups around the country.

This section of the *Lyme Disease Update* reports on their achievements and objectives on the federal and state levels. Common goals center on:

(1) Increasing awareness of the spread of Lyme and other tick-borne diseases;

(2) Spotlighting the need for further scientific research on the uncertainties in diagnosis, treatment, and prognosis at this point in the history of Lyme disease;

(3) Helping patients find effective care;

(4) Prevention.

Assisting patients, the third goal, includes promotion of an environment in which patients and doctors can freely pursue therapeutic options and reimbursement for long-term care of persistent Lyme disease.

---

2 Senate Committee on Administration, TX , *The prevalence of tick-borne illness in Texas: interim report*, November 2000, 77th Legislature.

POLITICAL ACTIVITY, FEDERAL GOVERNMENT

Congress

Both houses of Congress passed resolutions designating a "Lyme Disease Awareness Week" in 1989, 1990, 1991, 1993, and 1994. Congress passed the Food, Agriculture, Conservation, and Trade Act in 1990, authorizing $250,000 in each of the fiscal years 1991-95 for deer tick ecology and related research. These funds were for use by the Agricultural Research Service.

In 1994, initiated by Congressman Christopher Smith (NJ), the Department of Defense Appropriations Act authorized $1,000,000 for a Lyme disease research program to be utilized by the Army.

The Agricultural Research, Extension, and Education Reform Act of 1998 called for the Secretary of Agriculture to make grants extending research related to deer tick ecology.

In 1999, the Department of Defense Appropriations Act provided $3,000,000 for research and surveillance activities relating to Lyme and other tick-borne diseases. Senator Christopher Dodd (CT) and Congressman Christopher Smith (NJ) were the impetus for the Lyme provisions in this Act.

After requesting input from the LDA, LDF and other Lyme organizations, Congressman Christopher Smith (NJ) authored and introduced in the US House of Representatives the first con-gressional bill fully devoted to Lyme. Titled the "Lyme Disease Initiative Act of 1998" (LDI 98), it called for $120,000,000 over five years for establishment of programs reducing the incidence and prevalence of Lyme disease. These programs were to be carried out in the Department of Health and Human Services (HHS) by the CDC and NIH, with collaboration by the Secretaries of the HHS and the Department of Defense. Congressman Smith's bill also provided for an advisory task force with members drawn from the public and private sectors, including Lyme activist groups.

Introduced too late for passage in the 105th Congress, the House bill's chief findings and goals have reappeared in modified form in later House and Senate bills on Lyme and associated tick-borne diseases. Among the findings of the 1998 bill:

- According to the CDC, there has been a 32-fold increase in reported cases since 1982.
- Under-reporting is likely, since no reliable standardized diagnostic test is available.
- "Lyme disease costs our Nation at least $60,000,000 a year in direct medical costs for early, acute cases. The cost of chronic cases of the disease, as well as the costs of lost wages and productivity, are many times higher." (Finding 4).
- Many health-care providers lack the appropriate level of knowledge to diagnose Lyme accurately, particularly in non-endemic regions of the country.

Goals of the 1998 House bill included: reliable tests for diagnosis and determination of active infection; a better surveillance and reporting system; wider physician and public education; prevention of associated tick-borne diseases; development of indicators in the ten highest endemic states; and a task force to provide input into federal Lyme disease expenditures.

After considerable input from government agencies and Lyme advocacy groups around the country, Congressman Smith introduced a broader version of his Lyme initiative in 1999. This bill increased appropriations to $125,000,000 over five years, contained the original provisions involving the CDC, NIH, and Defense Department, again called for creation of an advisory task force, but added public education and basic research components concerning, respectively, the Departments of the Interior (parks) and Agriculture.

Congressman Smith reintroduced essentially the same bill in 2001, with more House co-sponsors, including: Pitts (PA); Maloney (CT); Gilman, Hinchey, and Townes (NY); Saxton (NJ); Delahunt (MA); Wolf (VA); and Traficant (OH). LDA was successful in obtaining signatures of almost 100 nationwide groups, unrelated to Lyme, in support of the bill (e.g., forestry and sports associations, PTAs).

In the US Senate, Senator Edward Kennedy (MA) conducted a hearing on Lyme disease in 1993. Initially, Kennedy invited representatives of university-based physicians. When Lyme activists got word of the hearing, however, they waged a determined, successful campaign to open the session to patients and physicians specializing in persistent cases.

In 1998, Senator Christopher Dodd (CT) introduced the first Senate bill on Lyme disease, Lyme Disease Initiative 98 (LDI), a companion to Congressman Smith's LDI 98. The next year, Senator Rick Santorum (PA) sponsored the companion bill to Smith's expanded LDI 99.

Then, in 2001, after discussion with the CT-based Lyme Disease Foundation (LDF), Senator Christopher Dodd (CT) introduced the Lyme and Infectious Disease Information and Fairness in Treatment bill (LIFT). LIFT centered on establishment of a Tick-Borne Disorders Advisory Committee, with Lyme patients and clinical researchers dominating its membership, but it provided little in the way of measurable goals. (Congressman Jim Greenwood (PA) introduced the House version).

The Lyme bills stalled due to lack of consensus. The CT-based Greenwich Lyme Disease Task Force (now Time For Lyme), the LDA, and a firm of legislative consultants hired by these Lyme groups assisted in the development and passage, along with other groups across the country, of a compromise bill. Dodd produced a Senate bill reconciling LIFT and LDI (as reintroduced in the House in 2001), which unanimously passed the Senate in 2002. Introduced in the Senate again in 2003 by Santorum and supported by Dodd, this reconciliation bill, S-1527, is currently under consideration in the Senate committee and has just been introduced in the House at publication time by Congresswoman Sue Kelly (NY).

Members of Congress occasionally sponsor public educational forums on Lyme disease in their home states and districts. To cite noteworthy meetings: Representative Christopher Smith hosted the first congressional panel discussion on Lyme in Wall Township,

NJ, in October 1992 with members of the CDC, physicians, activists and patients speaking. Representative Joseph Pitts presided over a conference on Lyme and other tick-borne diseases in Chester County, PA, in June 1999. Representatives James Langevin (RI) and Rob Simmons (CT) held an educational forum which featured Lyme clinicians, public health officials and advocates from several states in a discussion on the diagnosis and treatment of Lyme in Westerly, RI, in August 2002. The current president of the LDA was an invited speaker at each of these events.

Centers for Disease Control & Prevention (CDC)

After the spirochete responsible for Lyme disease had been identified, the CDC set about formulating surveillance criteria to determine where the disease was most prevalent. Recognizing that these criteria needed to be narrow in scope and that there were various problems in determining whether a patient has Lyme, the agency placed a statement on its website recommending that physicians not use the surveillance criteria for diagnostic purposes, but that physicians make a clinical diagnosis. http://www.cdc.gov/ncidod/dvbid/lyme/casedef2.htm. Testing should be used as an adjunct to support clinical diagnosis.

At a conference in Dearborn, MI, in 1996, the CDC reformulated its surveillance criteria, narrowing its definition further for serologic detection of *Borrelia burgdorferi* infection. This reformulation has led to a reduction in the reported case figures state by state.

A number of Lyme clinicians have pointed out that the two-step serologic requirement subsequently at the core of the CDC surveillance criteria can exclude patients who actually have Lyme. This requirement calls first for an ELISA test for indirect evidence of antibodies to *Bb*; then, only if the ELISA is positive or equivocal, it calls for Western blots for more definite evidence.

The CDC reliance on Lyme ELISAs is questionable. For example: studies by the College of American Pathologists have concluded that currently-marketed ELISA assays are not sensitive enough for accurate screening and should not be part of the CDC's two-tier approach to serologic testing.

While Western blots tend to be more reliable and specific (done in top grade labs by experienced staff), various factors must be weighed in evaluating them. Also, Western blots are open to interpretation, and this can vary with the interpreter.

Most importantly, the CDC's revision of its surveillance criteria restricted the number of bands indicative of Lyme on Western blots to five out of ten for IgG and two out of three for IgM, but other bands not included by the CDC can be indicative as well. As redefined in 1996, the CDC criteria exclude bands representing OspA and OspB, which are very specific for Bb and therefore significant in detecting Lyme.

IgM bands are used to help diagnose Lyme in the early acute stage, IgG bands are used to help diagnose Lyme in later stages. Note, however, that IgM bands can be important indicators after a month; in persistent Lyme, the IgG response frequently is not fully positive, and only the IgM response remains. (About a third of all Lyme patients test IgG negative during the first year.)

Bottom line on serologic assays: The ELISAs and Western blots required for surveillance by the CDC miss patients with Lyme disease. Further, while the numbers can only be estimated, the CDC's two-step serologic requirement demonstrably contributes to a general under-reporting of cases in the US. An explanation of the complications and inadequacies of serologic testing can be read in the Introduction to the LDA *Update*.

In addition to the problems with ELISAs and Western blots, Lyme clinicians question whether the CDC surveillance criteria are at variance with recent research on differences in the ticks and spirochete species involved in human infection. An example follows.

For surveillance purposes, the CDC requires microscopic corroboration of *Bb* spirochetes from the margins of an EM rash before accepting Lyme cases outside three regions in the US–the northeast, part of the upper midwest, and CA and OR. In these three regions, where the agency credits reports lacking microscopic evidence, *Ixodes* ticks (deer ticks) are known to be endemic vectors for Lyme, and the spirochete appears to be predominantly the *Bb* species, identified in the early1980s.

In regions that the CDC does not consider endemic for Lyme, the agency's insistence on microscopic evidence has led to the categorization of a tick-borne infection as a "Lyme-like" condition that the CDC calls STARI, southern tick-associated rash illness— others call it Masters'Disease.

Dr. Edwin Masters has documented hundreds of these cases in Missouri (outside the US regions regarded as endemic by the CDC). These cases fit diagnostic criteria for Lyme disease, but he hasn't been able to culture spirochetes in the growth medium specified by the CDC. Generally, except for spirochetes from EM lesions, culturing spirochetes from human tissue has met with limited success. If Masters' pathogen is a different species, this might explain his difficulty in culturing it.

At first, the CDC routinely rejected his reports for lack of microscopic proof. Masters responded by repeatedly publishing his data in peer-reviewed journals. Repeatedly, the CDC countered that these data suggested a "Lyme-like" illness.

Lately, the CDC has placed Masters' cases in a separate category of tick-borne disease, caused, according to the agency, not by the *Bb* spirochete but by another *Borrelia* species, which produces Lyme-like manifestations treatable by antibiotics. The CDC has named this pathogen *B. lonestari*, after the lone star tick, *Amblyomma americanum*, its vector. The first culture isolation from a tick line in MN now indicates that this is a different species of *Borrelia* which produces Lyme[2a]. The lone star tick coexists with the deer tick, *Ixodes scapularis,* in Missouri, as it does in most states including those along the eastern seaboard.

Apply the illustration supplied by Masters to other Missouri doctors, and to doctors in other states where the species of spirochete and ticks differ from those satisfying the CDC reporting

---

[2a] Varela, A et al, The first culture isolation of B. lonestari, putative agent of southern tick-associated rash illness, Mar. 2004;1163-69.

criteria, and a picture emerges of likely widespread under-reporting of diseases caused by *Bb* and related *Borrelia* spirochetes.[2b]

The CDC awards community-based grants periodically to states to study the control of tick vectors and CT and NJ received grants in 2004 for such projects.

Food & Drug Administration (FDA)

A "Public Health Advisory: Limitations, Use, and Interpretation of Assays for Supporting Clinical Diagnosis of Lyme Disease," issued by the FDA in 1997,[3] addressed commonly-marketed assays for detecting antibodies to *Borrelia burgdoreri*, the spirochete causing Lyme disease. The results of these serologic tests, the FDA warned, "may easily be misinterpreted."

Physicians should use the assays "only to support a clinical diagnosis," recommended the FDA. In discussing the results of ELISA tests (also EIA and IFA tests), diagnosticians must bear in mind, the agency stressed, that "a negative result should not be the basis for excluding *Bb* as the cause of illness, especially if blood was collected within 2 weeks of when symptoms began." The FDA virtually repeated this ELISA advisory for Western blots in its discussion of the follow up Western blots.

Comparison of the FDA's strong 1997 advisory with public position statements by the CDC over the years suggests that the FDA may have felt an urgent need to state its position publicly on serologic assays for Lyme because of substantial misuse or misunderstanding by physicians of the CDC's two-tier antibody testing system. This testing system, at the core of the CDC surveillance criteria, is to be used for cases to meet the CDC surveillance criteria, which again, are not for diagnostic purposes.

[2b] Scoles G et al, A relapsing fever group spirochete transmitted by *Ixodes scapularis* tick, *Vector Borne and Zoonotic Diseases*, Vol.1, Num.1, 2001; 21-34. According to a press release by one of the authors, Durland Fish, Yale, the research in this article documents the existence of a previously unrecognized and yet un-named Borrelia species transmitted by *Ixodes* ticks found in up to 20% of infected ticks in RI, CT, NY, NJ, and he says there is no way to diagnose it.

[3] FDA Advisory, *JAMA*, September 10, 1997-Vol 278, No. 10

A public hearing on LYMErix™, a commercially-developed vaccine for Lyme disease, held by the FDA in May 1998 to consider marketing, ended with a narrow vote for approval; however, it produced so many reservations about safety that the committee chairperson remarked: "It is fairly rare for a vaccine to be voted on with so much ambivalence by everyone with a stack of provisos."[4]

Subsequently, the manufacturer marketed and distributed approximately 1.4 million doses of vaccine between December 1998 and October 2000. During this period, the FDA received reports of 1,048 adverse events (0.07 percent of the doses)[5]

These adverse effects prompted the FDA to hold a vaccine advisory committee hearing in 2002. Public testimony at this hearing, including that from people in wheelchairs claiming to be injured by the vaccine, moved the FDA to urge the vaccine manufacturer to complete follow-up studies on safety. LDA testified at this hearing.

In January 2002, at LDA's request, the FDA held a private meeting with the Lyme Disease Association to review concerns raised by continued distribution of the vaccine. NJ Congressman Christopher Smith was instrumental in ensuring that the session took place as scheduled. The LDA took a doctor and a consultant acquainted with OspA-based vaccines to the meeting, and it had previously submitted a list of written questions to the FDA to be answered at the meeting.

A month later, the manufacturer quietly pulled LYMErix™ from the market, citing poor sales. (The written answers to the questions LDA presented to FDA were faxed to LDA three days prior to the manufacturer's withdrawal of the vaccine from the market.)

National Aeronautics and Space Administration (NASA)

NASA has invented the rotating wall vessel bioreactor to culture bacteria. It spins and neutralizes most of gravity's effects and

---

[4] Lyme Disease Association, *Conflicts of interest in Lyme disease: laboratory testing, vaccination, and treatment guidelines*, 2001

[5] Lymerix®Safety Data Reported to the Vaccine Adverse Event Reporting System www.fda.gov

encourage cells to grow in a natural manner. As cells replicate in this environment, which simulates natural conditions, they can "communicate" how they should grow, what is nearby, and how they should respond. *Borrelia burgdorfei*, along with Human immunodeficiency virus (HIV) and Ebola virus, are the infectious organisms being studied using the new technology.

NASA also funded research that includes remote-sensing maps to detect global epidemics for diseases such as malaria and Lyme.

National Institutes of Health (NIH)

Organized political activity by patients has helped the NIH appreciate the need for government-supported studies where questions about the cause, diagnosis, and treatment of Lyme disease remain unresolved.

The National Institute of Allergies and Infectious Diseases (NIAID) has funded several clinical trials on Lyme. Reports about a few trials appeared in the July 12, 2001 issue of the *New England Journal of Medicine.*

One report, by Nadelman et al, discussed the prophylactic efficacy of a single dose of doxycycline after a tick bite, endorsing such a regimen. The Nadelman team used the EM rash as a primary endpoint, evaluated subjects for six weeks, and their results (showing possible benefits) had a 95% confidence interval of 25-98%.

Nadelman's study has not fostered a consensus of expert opinion about its value. There was a wide margin of error in the confidence level, the evaluative period may have been too short to assess the development of persistent infection due to resistant *Bb*, and an EM rash may not present in some cases.

The other report, by Klempner et al, concerned a study of antibiotic therapy for patients with a history of Lyme disease who had developed symptoms of chronic Lyme despite earlier antibiotic therapy. Specifically, Klempner's team compared treatment with IV ceftriaxone for 30 days followed by oral doxycyline for 60 days to IV placebo, followed by oral placebo for the same duration.

Klempner et al found no statistically significant difference between the group receiving antibiotics and the group given placebo in the trials. These findings have also not fostered a consensus of opinion among the clinical research community. To cite two reservations: clinical experience suggests that Lyme patients sick enough to require IV antibiotics may not respond to one month of treatment, and adding oral antibiotics for two more months may not benefit them either.

In 1999, two years before publication of the Nadelman and Klempner reports, the NIH-NIAID granted 4.7 million dollars to a research team at Columbia University, headed by Dr. Brian Fallon, to conduct functional brain imaging and evaluate treatment in patients with chronic neuropsychiatric Lyme disease.

Fallon's study, nearing completion, has enrolled patients between the ages of 18 to 65 from an extended geographical range. Entry criteria include: a well documented history of Lyme disease, at least three weeks of IV antibiotic treatment, and persistent problems with memory. (See the Introduction for the import of Fallon's study and a seed grant by the LDA enabling Fallon to supply preliminary data to the NIH.)

US Department of Agriculture (USDA).

In 1997, the Department of Agriculture implemented a 5-year tick control research project in four areas of the northeastern US where the incidence of Lyme disease is among the highest in the country. In these areas, feeding bins for the white-tailed deer that serve as the adult Lyme tick's main animal host have been designed so that each of the four corners of the bin has a paint roller containing an acaricide.

Lured by whole-kernel corn in the bins, the deer brush against the rollers and the acaricide rubs off, killing ticks on the animals' head and neck, where 90% of the adult Lyme ticks are found. As the deer groom themselves, they spread the acaricide to other areas of the body. The particular acaricide used targets ticks without harming beneficial insects. (The EPA has just approved this deer feeder station for public use, through the American Lyme Disease Foundation, ALDF, although state approvals may vary.)

For persons working or playing in wooded places, the Department of Agriculture's Forest Service provides Internet links informing the public of precautions that can prevent tick bites. These links also supply information on the manifestations of Lyme and other diseases spread by ticks, especially babesiosis and Ehrlichiosis.

The LDA contributed funds to the USDA in 2001 toward development by the Department of Agriculture of a natural means of tick control. Nematodes (threadlike worms) were tried in field trials on *Ixodes* and *Amblyomma* ticks. They proved effective in killing adult female ticks in the field and had a significant impact on the number of larval ticks in the environment. The studies are ongoing, testing various nematode strains and further refining the procedures for application.

Occupational Safety & Health Administration (OSHA)

Responding to inquiries on occupational exposure to ticks transmitting Lyme disease, OSHA put out a "Hazard Information Bulletin" in April 2000 (see website). The bulletin provided guidance to workers in grassy or densely forested areas on how to decrease the risk of becoming infected.

Included in the information in OSHA's lengthy bulletin were the following points:

- "The CDC estimates that the number of annually reported cases of Lyme disease has increased 33-fold since national surveillance began in 1982.
- "In 1998, the estimated incidence of Lyme disease was about 6 per 100,000 people in the US; however, there may be considerable under-reporting.
- "Communications with the Vaccine Adverse Events Reporting System (VAERS) Hotline during September 1999 indicated that some reports of adverse events relating to LYMErix have been made.
- "Lyme disease vaccine does not protect all recipients against infection with *B. burgdorferi* and offers no protection against other tick-borne diseases."

POLITICAL ACTIVISM, STATES

Once the non-profit Lyme Disease Association of NJ significantly expanded its scope in 1999, becoming the Lyme Disease Association (LDA), a national non-profit organization, the LDA gained affiliates and opened chapters in ten states. Currently, groups in other states are expressing interest in joining with the LDA.

Note that the states and activities given coverage in the *Update* mainly illustrate educational and advocacy efforts resulting in the passage of legislation, or the introduction of bills presently awaiting passage, and the establishment of government-fostered advisory panels on Lyme. These activities also include successful efforts to obtain legislative and administrative mandates for reimbursement for treatment, the collection of data on Lyme incidence, and programs for education and prevention.

For the most part, the efforts covered here are recent. In several instances, they involve hearings on Lyme by committees of the state legislature and members of the executive branch of the state government, policy discussions with government officials, and other activity of a political nature scheduled to occur in 2004.

California

Political interaction in California grew out of a determination by Lyme disease patients to educate physicians and the public about this tick-borne infection. To achieve this goal, patients and their families in the counties of Sonoma, Mendocino, Marin, and later Trinity, coalesced into ad hoc committees in the late 1980s.

Feature stories on Lyme in the national print media led to the introduction of a Lyme bill in the state legislature as early as the fall of 1990. In 1998, the first CA bill passed into law created the Lyme Disease Advisory Committee. This body remains active; California's recent budgetary crisis, however, has limited it to one meeting a year.

At the turn of the millennium the Lyme Disease Resource Center, publisher of the national *Lyme Times*, had emerged as the foremost advocacy group in the state. It affiliated with LDA in 2002 and has since changed its name to the California Lyme Disease Association (CALDA).

CALDA had input into a workers' compensation law passed in 2002. Its provisions apply to employees of the California Conservation Corps and members of certain law enforcement agencies whose outdoor duties result in their becoming infected by Lyme.

Preliminary data from an ongoing CALDA national patient survey, have shown to date that 67% of respondents were delayed in their diagnosis of Lyme disease because of misapplication of the CDC surveillance criteria (either ELISA or Western blot) as diagnostic criteria. The average number of years of delay in diagnosis has been 3.18. Final results will be published.

In March 2004, CALDA saw its activism efforts bear fruit, as California became the first western state to hold hearings on Lyme disease, through the CA Senate Health Committee.

Connecticut

In 1975 Polly Murray, an artist in Lyme, CT, whose young son had developed arthritis, learned of other cases of childhood arthritis in Lyme and neighboring towns. She reported these cases to the CT Health Department and to physicians specializing in epidemiology and rheumatology at Yale University. The Yale researchers studied the cases, concluded that they represented a distinct new illness, which they labeled "Lyme arthritis, and published the first modern description of this condition in the US medical literature.

Organized activity by Lyme patients and their families started early in 1988. Polly Murray and other mothers of children with Lyme formed the Lyme Disease Awareness Task Force.

That same year, the Lyme Borreliosis Foundation (LBF), subsequently the Lyme Disease Foundation (LDF), was formed. Early efforts by these groups centered on educating the public about Lyme. Later, the LDF held medical conferences to educate physicians. It also started a peer-reviewed medical journal devoted to Lyme and its associated tick-borne diseases.

In 1998 mothers of Greenwich children suffering from late symptoms of Lyme held a public forum with the Greenwich Department of Health. They set up an informal task force, including a representative of the Greenwich Department of Health, and held educational sessions with physicians and researchers specializing in Lyme.

Early in 1999 this informal task force invited the LDA to a private meeting in Greenwich with CT Attorney General Richard Blumenthal, who had received letters from Lyme patients denied reimbursement for long-term treatment. As requested, the LDA presented a history of government activity on Lyme disease in NJ. Insurance coverage and diagnostic and treatment problems then dominated the discussion. By year's end, the task force had formally organized into the Greenwich Lyme Disease Task Force (GLDTF).

Soon afterward, Blumenthal conducted a hearing on Lyme in Hartford, the state capital, in 1999. He then proposed a bill mandating full coverage for Lyme disease treatment. This bill, which became law later in 1999, contained restrictions added by legislators in passage: Insurers would henceforth pay for 30 days of IV antibiotics, 60 days of oral antibiotics; patients requiring longer antibiotic therapy, however, would have to obtain approval from either a neurologist, rheumatologist, or infectious disease specialist.

Problems relating to the restrictions on coverage arose. The crucial one: Patients needing longer treatment were having difficulty finding the required specialists needed to and willing to approve the treatment. This problem was especially evident in the area of pediatrics where these specialists were scarce. The AG has held community meetings to try and resolve the problems and help patients get necessary treatment.

Around this time until 2003, the Wilton Lyme Disease Task Force formed, devoting time to education issues and fundraising for research and education.

A year later, the LDA and GLDTF arranged a meeting with the Commissioner of the CT Department of Health, Joxel Garcia,

Attorney General Blumenthal, and CT advocacy groups. The meeting aimed to widen regional awareness of concerns about Lyme and to address regulatory issues raised by physicians offering long-term antibiotic treatment.

By 2001, the GLDTF had affiliated with the LDA. Its activities now mostly centered on raising funds for Lyme disease research and educating the public and government officials about problems arising from Lyme and its co-infections. GLDTF and TFL joined forces to partner with Columbia University to open an endowed research center at Columbia. In 2003, the GLDTF changed its name to Time For Lyme (TFL).

In 2003, CERCLD, the Committee for Education Reform for Children with Lyme Disease, formed. Together with LDA and TFL, CERCLD met with the CT State Department of Education and presented possible curriculum and other ideas to be adopted by the State. TFL had already developed initiatives being used in the Greenwich schools.

Attorney General Blumenthal and Dr. J. Robert Galvin, the new health commissioner, conducted a second hearing on Lyme in January 2004. The use of the surveillance criteria was a prime issue on the agenda. Also high on the agenda: a decision by the CT Department of Health in 2003 to drop mandatory laboratory reporting of Lyme disease in CT. Up to 80% of cases reported had originated with labs, but only 20% of case reports had come from physicians.

The CT Lyme Disease Coalition (CLDC) formed to support Blumenthal's second hearing. It included most CT Lyme groups and the LDA. The CLDC met with Blumenthal and Galvin in the spring of 2004 to reemphasize hearing concerns and ask for specific health department actions such as letters to CT doctors telling them not to use CDC surveillance criteria for diagnosis, reinstatement of mandatory lab reporting of Lyme cases, and implementation of Lyme disease programs in the schools.

Other noteworthy active task forces in CT include those in Newtown who recently sponsored an educational forum with their Rotary that drew over 300 people to hear a doctor and the LDA speak about Lyme issues, and newly formed Ridgefield, where the First Selectman held a community forum moderated by LDA–the response to the forum precipitated the task force formation. Also, Dolly Curtis Interviews has produced numerous educational videos featuring physicians knowledgable about Lyme disease. LDA has supported several of the productions.

Delaware

In the spring of 2003, the LDA held an educational forum to raise awareness about Lyme and help organize activity by Delaware patients and Lyme advocates. The LDA, Delaware Chapter, formed at the year's end. It has since been developing initiatives for educational programs on Lyme disease and has planned its first fundraiser for Lyme disease research in the summer of 2004.

Thanks to DE State Senator Karen Peterson and Deleware Lyme Support, the DE Senate passed a Resolution to Create a Lyme Disease Task Force in DE.

Iowa

The Lyme Disease Association of Iowa will be meeting with US Senator Harkin's office, the State Insurance Commissioner, Teri Vaughan, and state Senator Lisa Heddens. In the fall, the group has plans to meet with the head of the IA Medical Society.

Kansas

Advocacy on behalf of KS and MO Lyme patients has been spearheaded by the Lyme Association of Greater Kansas City, which affiliated with the LDA in 2002. In 2004, this organization submitted a written presentation on Lyme disease to the KS House Health Committee. Additionally, this group supplied packets of information on Lyme and its associated tick-borne diseases to nurses in KS schools, and it has supported the EICS conferences (see MO). LDA spoke at EICS in 2003.

Massachusetts

Groups representing Lyme patients, including members of the MA Lyme Disease Coalition, have been consulted or included in meetings of officials of the Massachusetts Department of Health going back at least to 1998. As part of their regular duties, epidemiologists in this department had been tracking the number of cases county by county since 1985, finding a continual increase, for instance: 315 statewide in 1997, 738 in 1998, 1789 in 2002. The highest incidence figures have come from Cape Cod and surrounding islands in the east, and the second highest (lately) from Berkshire County in the west; but every county in Massachusetts has now reported Lyme disease.

From the late 1990s a committee composed of Department of Health staff and members of local advocacy groups has advised the Department of Health on development of Lyme policy and programs. The committee, not funded by the state, has met three or four times per year. It has assisted in designing a case report form for Lyme and a physicians' reference manual, "Tick-Borne Diseases In Massachusetts."

A state legislator hosted a forum on Lyme disease in MA in 2002. The LDA appeared at the legislator's invitation and made a presentation at this forum.

In 2003 the LDA formed the LDA Cape Cod Chapter, which has centered its activity on educational programs in schools.

Michigan

A CDC grant of $245,000 to assist deer tick research in Upper Michigan initiated government action on Lyme here. Given in 1989, the grant provided funds through 1995. At that time, the Michigan Health Department held that no Lyme disease existed in the lower portion of the state.

Activity on behalf of Lyme patients began in Saginaw, in lower eastern MI, in 1990 with formation of the MI Lyme Disease Association. A group called the Lyme Alliance, in Jackson (lower MI), set up an Internet web site in 1995, and published a bimonthly national newsletter (through 2004). The Lyme Alliance also submitted an *amicus* brief on behalf of a physician charged with improperly treating Lyme disease. (See the Law section of this *Update*, under "State Medical Boards.")

Two hearings involving Lyme were conducted by the Michigan House of Representatives in 1996. L. Brooks Patterson, the father of a Lyme patient, and Health Commissioner of Oakland County, MI, interested the Legislature in holding these hearings.

At the hearings, Lyme patients questioned the state health department's contention that lower Michigan showed no evidence of infected ticks. Finally, in 2003 the health department reversed its position, disclosing that infected ticks had, in fact, been found there.

Minnesota

Organized educational and political activity in this upper mid-western state date to the formation of the nonprofit Lyme Disease Coalition of MN (LDCMN), October 1991. The LDCMN sponsored three seminars at hospitals in Minneapolis and St. Paul in 1992, 1993, and 1994. These were concerned with educating the public and government about Lyme, the need for further Lyme research, and ways to help families cope with infected family members.

Once the LDCMN and other advocacy groups made legislators aware of the hardships resulting from Lyme, bills were introduced into both houses of the legislature in 1995 and 1996. The first would have created literature on preventing Lyme to be distributed in state parks and hunting areas. The second would have provided diagnostic and treatment guidelines for physicians dealing with Lyme cases. For various reasons, neither passed into law.

A rider concerning Lyme was attached to a bill on pregnancy and did become law in 1996. The rider mandates insurance coverage for diagnosis and forbids restrictions on preventive care. Insurance companies, however, have avoided reimbursement for IV treatment by claiming it is neither medically necessary nor proven effective.

In 1998, a Lyme bill passed both houses of the legislature, allowing physicians to determine appropriate treatment for patients and mandating insurance coverage; but Blue Cross of MN challenged the act in the state court, keeping it from going into effect.

Missouri

A fully-accredited medical conference on Lyme disease has been held annually in Missouri for years, sponsored by an organization known as the Emerging Infectious Diseases of the Central States (EICS). This state has also been the focus of a medical dispute between the CDC and Lyme specialist Dr. Edwin Masters over the identity of the tick serving as the vector for an illness with virtually the same manifestations as Lyme, caused by a different species of *Borrelia* spirochete. (See the subsection above on the CDC.)

New Jersey

Among the very first states to act on Lyme disease in response to constituent concern, New Jersey has a lengthy history of legislative and administrative interaction with Lyme patients and advocates. Formed in 1988 and incorporated in1990, the LDA of Northern New Jersey (LDANNJ) began to work with the 1992 incorporated LDA of Central Jersey (LDACJ), and the newly created Lyme Disease Coalition (LDC),which would be a liaison to public officials. They and other NJ Lyme activists, began educating legislators about the public health problems arising from Lyme.

By 1993, the LDACJ filed a name change and along with LDANNJ, became the Lyme Disease Association of New Jersey (LDANJ), which was concentrating on raising monies for Lyme research, helping children in schools, and on gaining public input in government decisions on Lyme policy. The New Jersey Lyme Committee (NJLC) also formed at this time to help shape the political agenda of Lyme disease in NJ.

In 1992, then Wall Township Board of Education member Pat Smith presented a study of Lyme disease in nine NJ school districts to the CDC and NIH at a meeting in DC hosted by Congressman Christopher Smith. As a result, the CDC came to NJ and performed a follow-up study in five of the school districts: several conclusions from the unpublished CDC study were that the median duration of illness at the time of interview was 363 days, the mean number of school days missed because the child was too ill to attend was 103 days, and according to 78% of the parents, children experienced a fall in grade point average during the time of illness.

In 1993, the LDANJ, and the LDC succeeded in getting the first Lyme law on the books. The law established the (NJ) Governor's Lyme Disease Advisory Council, GLDAC the first in the nation, which today continues to apprise the Governor of problems relating to Lyme in NJ. The current LDA president was GLDAC chair in 1997.

Also in 1993, the LDANJ and the NJLC and VOICE (Victims of Insurance Company Exploitation), joined forces to have bills introduced that required insurers to cover Lyme patients' long-term treatments in both houses of the legislature. State house rallies, candlelight vigils and picketing helped to define the issue. The first such bills in the US, they passed both houses, but one of the sponsors had made changes to his bill which he refused to reconcile, and the session ended without adoption into law. Since then, the bill mandating insurance coverage for physician-diagnosed treatment has been introduced during every legislative session. In 2004, both houses introduced the bill (sponsors Assemblyman Christopher Connors and Senator Barbara Buono), and as of press time, LDA and the Greater Raritan Group are meeting with legislators to discuss the issues surrounding bill passage.

A 1995 bill, initiated by the LDANJ, did pass into law. It mandated annual teacher in-service education for teachers with students having Lyme disease. It also required formulation of a Lyme curriculum, which the NJ State Department of Education adopted for school grades K-12. The law recommended that districts in Lyme endemic areas adopt the curriculum for use. That same year, the LDANJ hosted the first of a series of a half dozen statewide forums on Lyme disease for educators featuring speakers such as Dr. Brian Fallon from Columbia University.

In 1997, the "Vector Control Bill," supported by the LDANJ, became law. It provided for each county to decide on the agency to deal with ticks; most counties placed tick control under their existing Mosquito Control Commission.

Also in 1997, the LDANJ arranged a meeting with then State Senator James McGreevey's office. The session familiarized McGreevey with the difficulties experienced by NJ patients: getting diagnosed and treated for Lyme and reimbursed for Lyme disease treatment. In 2003, now Governor McGreevey in a letter to the organizations, commended LDA and its CT affiliate, TFL, for their commitment and affiliation with Columbia University to fund and open a research center for chronic Lyme disease at Columbia. (Almost half the monies have been committed to date).

In 1998, the LDANJ hosted a Lyme disease forum for federal officials, featuring physicians speaking to educate the NJ congressional delegation; most offices sent representatives. US Representative Robert Andrews (NJ) was a featured speaker.

NJ gave birth to a number of Internet sites. In 1994, the Lyme Disease Network of New Jersey developed one of the first extensive Internet web sites in the world, www.Lymenet.org, dedicated to public education of the prevention and treatment of Lyme disease and other tick-borne illnesses. It became an affiliate of the LDA in the year 2000. The Lyme Disease Audio Network, also operating from NJ, has recordings of Lyme doctors and advocates that can be accessed online at www.Lymediseaseaudio.com.

NJ has the dubious distinction of being perhaps the first state in the nation to have its medical board charge a physician in connection with Lyme treatment in 1990. In 1999, Congressman Christopher Smith, whose district is endemic for Lyme, and the LDA(NJ), each met with the NJ State Board of Medical Examiners, SBME. Congressman Smith and the LDA were concerned about the Board's investigations of physicians offering long-term antibiotic therapy for Lyme.

A March 2000 letter to the SBME from Congressman Smith states in part: "In cases of Lyme disease, however, two physicians could examine the same patient's set of symptoms and come away with totally different diagnoses. Moreover, two sets of Eliza and western Blot tests could be run on the same samples, and two different sets of results can be recorded....Even if both physicians managed to agree that the patient had Lyme disease, they could easily disagree over the length of time to treat the patient...Both could cite peer reviewed studies published in respectable medical journals to back up each person's scientific viewpoint. The challenge with Lyme disease as I see it, is that the State Board of Medical Examiners has a responsibility to make certain that in the course of investigating complaints about Lyme disease treatment, the Board does not inadvertently prosecute physicians merely for holding legitimate scientific differences of opinion." Since those meetings, the state medical board appears to have pursued few, if any, such investigations.

On another policy matter, a broad regional approach to Lyme disease, the LDA, inviting affiliate groups from nearby states, met with NJ Senior Assistant Commissioner, James Blumenstock, and the state epidemiologist, Dr. Eddy Breznitz, in 2001. The LDA pointed out that a number of northeastern states have problems in common dealing with Lyme and that coordinated policy and programs should make for more effective management.

To date, the Lyme Disease Association has been successful in raising over $2 million for Lyme disease research, education and prevention. It has held four fully accredited medical conferences for physicians and funded research projects coast to coast, with institutions ranging from Columbia University to University of Medicine & Dentistry of New Jersey to Fox Chase Cancer Center to University of California, Davis. A number of the LDA-funded projects have been published in peer-reviewed journals including *JAMA*. It has affiliates and/or chapters in 10 states.

At press time, LDA received a response letter from the Department of Health & Senior Services (DHSS) concerning DHSS's new 2004 CDC community grant. In it, DHSS touts the completion of a three-year prevention program in Morris and Somerset Counties, and indicates the data, still being analyzed, will hopefully provide prevention information usable in NJ and the Northeast.

New York

This state is traditionally number one in reported cases, so it is not surprising that one of the earliest groups in the country that was active on behalf of Lyme patients was the Westchester Lyme Disease Support Group. Later, the Lyme Disease Coalition of NY/CT formed, and the notable grass roots organization, Voices of Lyme NY/Lyme, which has spurred much political activity in NY.

Stop Ticks On People (STOP) formed in NY in 2001–created on the recommendation of the Dutchess County Legislative Task Force to Study Tick Control to form an organization that would carry on and expand upon its mission. STOP operates as a coalition in partnership with The United Way of Dutchess County and various other organizations including the LDA. All are united to reduce the incidence of tick-borne disease through education, awareness and prevention.

Attempting to speed OPMC, Office of Professional Medical Conduct, reform, NY Assembly members invited the LDA and the Hudson Valley Lyme Disease Committee to several meetings with representatives of Governor George Pataki's office and meetings with officials of the OPMC in 2001-2. OPMC was targeting physicians who treat chronic Lyme disease.

Hearings by the NY Assembly Health Committee in November 2001 (Albany) and January 2002 (NYC) examined, respectively, Lyme diagnosis and treatment and the lack of due process in the Office of Professional Medical Conduct (OPMC), the NY agency that disciplines MDs.

Testimony at these all-day sessions ranged over many issues, and during the 2002 hearing, witnesses alleged due process abuses by the OPMC that go well beyond those singled out by Lyme patients, physicians, and advocates. Independent groups, notably the Bar Association of the State of NY, criticized the OPMC on due process and suggested reforms. The LDA testified by invitation at both hearings.

In the Assembly, these hearings and meetings led to an OPMC reform bill in 2002. The bill adds due process in the investigation of all physicians, including standardization of the introduction of peer-review to support treatment practices. The bill overwhelmingly passed, but the Senate took no action. In 2003, the OPMC reform bill (Richard Gottfried, Chair, Assembly Health Committee, NY) passed the Assembly, and Senator Seward introduced the bill in the Senate in 2004.

Assemblywoman Nettie Mayersohn, who has been active along with Assemblyman Joel Miller on behalf of Lyme patients, introduced a bill in 2003, which passed the Assembly in 2004, expanding due process rights for physicians who treat chronic Lyme disease patients. It includes a provision to enable the doctor to know the identity of expert witnesses in a timely fashion and another which reveals the identity of the complainant if other than a patient. Senator Vincent Leibell has introduced the Senate version.

One recent OPMC prosecution of a Lyme specialist using long-term treatment, the case of Dr. Joseph Burrascano, ended with noteworthy opinions by the hearing panel and the administrative review board (ARB). Other state medical boards might review them before considering action against physicians who treat chronic Lyme. The panel said (and in essence the ARB agreed):

"The Hearing Committee recognizes the existence of the current debate within the medical community over issues concerning management of patients with recurrent or long term Lyme disease. This appears to be a highly polarized and politicized conflict, as was demonstrated to this Committee by expert testimony from both sides, each supported by numerous medical journal articles, and each emphatic that the opposite position was clearly incorrect. In fact, it often appeared that the testimony was framed to espouse specific viewpoints, rather than directly answer questions posed. What clearly did emerge, however, was that Respondent's approach, while certainly a minority viewpoint, is one that is shared by many other physicians. We recognize that the practice of medicine may not always be an exact science, 'issued guidelines' are not regulatory, and patient care is frequently individualized. We are also acutely aware that it was not this Committee's role to resolve this medical debate."[6]

---

[6] NY, Board of Professional Medical Conduct, Burrascano, BPMC #01-265.

NY also has two bills mandating insurance coverage for Lyme disease: introduced by Assemblyman Thiele (insurance and worker's compensation) and Senator Trunzo (not identical to Assembly version).

North Carolina

Organized political activity has made headway in this state under leadership of the newly formed North Carolina Lyme Disease Foundation (NCLDF). Currently, the focus is on collecting letters from patients testifying to the hardships resulting from Lyme. The NCLDF has scheduled a meeting with a member of the North Carolina General Assembly in 2004, where it will present these letters as a means of raising government awareness about the impact of Lyme.

Pennsylvania

On invitation, thanks to work of the LDA's PA Chapter (LDAPAC), the LDA and LDAPAC briefed the majority caucus of the PA House of Representatives in the state capital, Harrisburg, on various aspects of Lyme disease in 2001. Lyme & Associated Diseases of the Brandywine Valley also attended to help educate.

As the disease spread, central PA activists formed Ticked Off and Fed Up to raise awareness for the disease.

Several state representatives held forums on Lyme between 2002 and 2003. The Central PA Lyme Disease Support Group (CPLDSG) participated in organizing the forums. The LDA was an invited speaker at these events.

Two bills introduced in the legislature in 2003 were referred to committees for further action in 2004. The first, introduced in the Senate in March, would provide for appropriations of funds for education, prevention, and treatment of Lyme disease.

The second bill was introduced in the Assembly in September after legislators invited input from the LDAPAC. This bill, adding "related tick-borne diseases" under its provisions for improvements in diagnosis and treatment, would also make it easier for physicians and osteopaths to offer long-term treatment in persistent cases by protecting them against investigation by the state medical board for utilizing this therapeutic approach. The CPLDSG is now working for passage of the bill.

In 2003, the LDA took on board another affiliate, the LDA of Southeastern PA, which has assumed responsibility for informing the public and government officials about Lyme in one of the most endemic regions of the US, Chester County. Two recent forums saw 400-500 people at each one.

Rhode Island

Representatives of the LDA and GLDTF, providing a physician and a researcher knowledgeable about Lyme disease, met with RI Health Director Patricia Nolan in 2001 and familiarized her with the plight of patients in RI who were not able to obtain treatment and also with tick infectivity rates in the state. They also met with US Senator Lincoln Chafee's office. (LDA had provided some funding for a tick control project in RI).

Second in reported cases per capita of Lyme in the US, Rhode Island residents face a disproportionately high risk of infection by Lyme and other tick-borne diseases. Several groups formed including the RI Coalition. Governor Lincoln Almond, recognizing the seriousness of the problem, had issued an executive order in November 2001, creating a Lyme Commission to study Lyme and its co-infections in RI. Two Lyme laws were passed in 2002 and 2003, and the Commission was instrumental in passage of both bills.

Officially titled "The Governor's Commission on Lyme Disease and Other Tick-Borne Infections," this 18-member body held two hearings in April 2002, receiving testimony from medical, environmental, public health experts, and advocates including LDA, and numerous patients. Soon after, the Governor's Commission developed and recommended legislation. State Senator Susan Sosnowski and State Representative Peter T. Ginaitt then sponsored the 2002 bills in the Legislature, and the LDA worked with the RI Coalition and other local Lyme groups to educate legislators about the necessity of the law. By unanimous vote in both houses, the bills passed in early June, with Joseph Larisa, Chief of Staff for Governor Almond, taking a leadership role in passage. LDA was invited by Governor Almond to speak at the signing ceremony in the capital.

"The Lyme Disease Diagnosis and Treatment Act" of 2002 basically prevents the RI Board of Medical Licensure and Discipline from prosecuting physicians solely because they prescribe or give long-term antibiotics for clinically-diagnosed Lyme–provided they document the diagnosis and treatment plan in the patient's medical record. The definition of Lyme disease in this law is broader than the CDC's surveillance definition.

The State of RI entered into an agreement with insurance carrier, BC/BS of RI, to ensure that all who needed long term treatment would be reimbursed. Unfortunately, patients were still not being reimbursed, necessitating the passage of another bill.

A major role in passage of the 2003 law was played by the LDA RI Chapter, organized earlier that year. Notably, this law mandates insurance coverage for long-term antibiotic therapy when the treating physician determines such therapy is medically necessary. The 2003 law, which took effect in 2004, contained a 1-year sunset provision. A new version of the act removing the sunset provision was signed into law by Governor Donald Carcieri on June 8, 2004, making RI the only state in the nation with such mandatory coverage.

LDA provided a Lyme disease in-service for the RI School Nurses Association in 2003.

Texas

Several groups of Texas patients and advocacy groups, especially the TX Lyme Coalition (TLC), contacted the Legislature and Lt. Governor in 1999 about the issues surrounding Lyme and other tock-borne diseases. The Lt. Governor requested the Senate Committee on Administration to conduct a study on these infections, focusing on prevention and treatment. State Senator Chris Harris, a Lyme patient, chaired the Committee.

Holding public hearings in Austin, March 16, 2000, and Fort Worth, May 9, 2000, the Committee gathered information for use in formulating legislative mandates and proposals. A variety of experts invited by the Committee testified on the diverse views related to diagnosis and treatment of Lyme and its associated infections. Patients and advocacy groups also testified. Subsequently, the Committee issued recommendations for educational and preventive programs, as well as recommendations for further research and development of reliable diagnostic tests.

"Most importantly," the Interim Report on these hearings stated, "The Committee learned of the profound effect on the lives of ordinary people and their families who are unfortunate enough to be devastated by tick-borne illnesses and the associated complications. In general, these stories provided by patients and their loved ones followed the same pattern. These people became sick, went misdiagnosed or undiagnosed for long periods of time, and sought help from multiple health care providers. Their lives were permanently altered by these diseases."

Recently, the Texas Lyme Disease Association organized as a non-profit group, following in the footsteps of the now inactive TLC. They have become the latest LDA affiliate, as of May 2004.

Wisconsin

Wisconsin is one of the areas outside the east coast that has had significant Lyme disease problems. Several education groups have been active there. In 1990, Wisconsin Cooperative Extension issued *A Wisconsin Meat Facts and Analysis* subtitled "Lyme Disease, Deer Hunting and Venison Safety." A quote from the flyer: "There is no evidence to date that the disease can be transmitted by handling venison or coming in contact with deer meat or blood, although hypothetically this would seem possible. Some people have suggested hunters and processors wear rubber gloves while dressing out deer carcasses as a precautionary measure. The main threat in working with venison comes from having the ticks transfer from deer to people." The flyer also addresses cooking any meat if the bacteria should survive in the raw meat of the deer: "...it would be destroyed by cooking to 160°F (medium degree of doneness) or higher.

Other States

Lyme activists have organized groups in some 40 states (including the District of Columbia): FL (one leader runs a large on-line support), AZ, ME (as the ticks spread north, this state has become more active), MD (many groups here are now having educational seminars), OH, SC, SD, AK (military support), AL, AR, GA, IL, IN, MS, ND, NE, NM, TN, VA and OR–one group here has applied for non-profit status. Their goals range from providing patient support to educating the public and government about Lyme, and encouraging state initiatives that address the manifold issues surrounding the diagnosis, prevention, and treatment of Lyme disease and its associated tick-borne diseases. At press time, patients held a forum in NH, and a VT group has planned a summer fundraiser for Lyme disease research through the LDA.

(Additional information: since Lyme is now one of the most prevalent vector-borne bacterial diseases in the world, groups are forming all over: Canada, England, Germany, Nederlands, France, Finland, Hungary, Switzerland, to name a few countries becoming active)

NOTE: Material from this section was obtained through extensive interviews with many Lyme advocates and some public health officials, their reports and websites. This section of the *Lyme Disease Update* does not cover all groups associated or involved with Lyme disease, particularly support groups and on-line groups whose work is invaluable to Lyme patients across the country. We apologize for omissions.

LEGAL SECTION

Lyme Disease Update:
Related Legal Developments

This section of the *Lyme Disease Update* separates recent legal developments related to Lyme disease into five areas of civil and administrative law: medical malpractice cases; actions by state medical boards to assure the quality of medical care provided by physicians; workers' compensation claims; cases alleging discrimination against individuals disabled by illness (particularly in educational institutions); and claims against insurers for reimbursement of treatment believed by physicians to be medically necessary.

Covered in each area are whether the governing statutes are federal, state, or both; where cases and claims are brought and heard; what rules of evidence and trial or hearing practice are followed; the standards applied in determining facts and reaching verdicts; and the possible influence of non-judicial factors in the disposition of cases and claims. Actual cases, used as instances where Lyme patients and physicians who treat long-term have prevailed, are summarized when available at the close of each area.

Most people do best relying on expert guidance to piece together how the American judicial system works, what specific matters each part of the system handles, and when it can resolve conflicting interests and problems poorly dealt with through the other government branches. The Lyme Disease *Update* acknowledges the assistance of lawyers in preparing this section, which is for information purposes only.

MEDICAL MALPRACTICE

Medical malpractice cases, or "negligence" cases, as they are sometimes termed, are tried in state and federal civil courts. Suits in federal court usually involve plaintiffs and defendants who don't live or do business in the same state.

Indispensable in starting a case in court is a claim of injury caused by a physician whose treatment departed from the community standard of care (the quality of medical care provided for a particular condition by other physicians in the same regional community).

The parties in a malpractice suit normally can choose to try the case before a judge alone or before a jury with a judge presiding. Juries are allowed to hear and weigh only evidence that pertains to the specific claim of injury.

Rules for conducting trials bar hearsay evidence (anyone or anything that cannot be examined and cross-examined). The burden of proof in reaching a verdict is a preponderance of the credible evidence.

Malpractice cases hinge on whether a physician departed from a community standard of practice. To help determine whether such a departure occurred and was the "proximate" cause of injury, medical authorities – qualified by the judge to testify – give their expert opinions. (A "proximate cause of injury" is not the sole cause: it is a significant one.)

Currently, two approaches to diagnosis and treatment are used in Lyme disease. Two sets of diagnostic and treatment guidelines, reflecting the different approaches, are available in the peer-reviewed literature. Thus, two community standards of practice exist. The main reasons for the dual standard: clinical researchers have yet to elucidate fully the pathogenesis of Lyme or to determine the optimal treatment for early and later-stage disease.

Physicians following the first approach give two to four weeks of antibiotic therapy for early infection, believing this regimen suffices in most cases. Physicians using the second approach give antibiotics four to six weeks, believing early infection may require more time to resolve.

In persistent or recurrent Lyme, some physicians in the first "school of thought" think that many patients who've received antibiotic treatment considered effective may develop a "post-Lyme syndrome." They view subsequent manifestations in the majority of these patients as an auto-immune reaction to therapy or to debris from Bb bacteria killed by antibiotics. Other physicians in the second "school of thought" feel that the clinical manifestations and data for these patients indicate active infection, and they give intensive and extensive antibiotics, often IV, finding that many patients with chronic manifestations respond to lengthy or repeated therapy.

Most doctors can defend their choice of treatment in court by showing that it met one of the two standards of community practice. Only when the medical treatment provided clearly deviates from both standards or no treatment is given though both standards of care should have been known, can a plaintiff in a Lyme case prevail.

In Murray v. Chesapeake Family Practice Group, two physicians belonging to the Elkton office of this Maryland-based HMO were sued for failure to diagnose Lyme disease in a 14-year-old boy. The HMO was named as well. The boy presented in April 1996 with numerous manifestations indicative of early Lyme, but during several repeat visits no lab tests were done to confirm infection. His mother phoned the HMO repeatedly, with little attention paid to her concerns. At the trial, testimony disclosed that none of the physicians employed in the HMO's three offices had received guidelines for diagnosing Lyme.

In August that same year, the boy suffered seizures, collapsed, and was admitted to a hospital, where staff doctors, considering his history and residence in an area endemic for Lyme ticks, ordered diagnostic tests. These were positive for Lyme. Additional testing showed that he had lost 29 IQ points since his first visit to the HMO.

A jury heard the case, decided in 2000, and held that one doctor failed to meet the community standard for diagnosis but found him not directly responsible for the teenager's physical problems. The jury also held the HMO liable. It exonerated the second doctor. The original award for damages totaled $3.2 million; the judge later reduced it to $1.7 million, because the initial amount exceeded the state cap. Of the reduced award, the highest ever in Cecil County (where the case was heard), $1.2 million went for loss of future earnings, the remainder to cover previous medical bills.[1]

In Bratt v. Laskas, MD, FL 4th District Court of Appeal, January term 2003, a child and his parents initiated a medical malpractice action against a pediatric gastroenterologist, among others, for failure to diagnose the child's medical condition as Lyme disease. The trial court entered summary judgment in favor of the gastroenterologist.

The Fourth District Court of Appeal reversed, holding that genuine issues of material fact existed precluding summary judgment on the issue of whether the gastroenterologist's failure to diagnose and treat Lyme disease was the proximate cause of the child's injury. The Court also held that a pediatrician was properly allowed to testify regarding the gastroenterologist's breach of standard of care.[1a]

---

[1] Hamilton C, The Whig, 12/20/00. On-line newspaper story about the Murray case in local paper, no title.

[1a] http://www.4dca.org/May2003/05-21-03/4D01-3386op.pdf

STATE MEDICAL BOARDS

Every state has at least one medical board empowered by state law to investigate complaints against physicians and discipline them for providing substandard care. Recommendations for discipline range from figurative slaps on the wrist to revocation of a physician's license to practice in the state.

Cases against physicians for professional misconduct originate from complaints for the most part, which state boards must investigate. The process for investigating complaints and determining if they are serious enough to warrant prosecution varies among the state boards, although not significantly. Once a physician is charged, a hearing panel, drawn from the medical board, meets to hear evidence and to reach findings of fact. Then, if the panel determines the physician acted negligently, incompetently, improperly, unethically, immorally, or under physical impairment, it recommends appropriate disciplinary action.

Administrative law permits the introduction of evidence in board disciplinary proceedings that would not be admissible in court, e.g. hearsay. Further, a claim of injury is not a prerequisite for investigation and trial by medical boards as it is in civil court malpractice cases. In other words, the boards can act to protect the public from exposure to medical care the boards believe might prove harmful. The burden of proof is similar to that in the civil court; a preponderance of the credible evidence (51%) is sufficient to support a finding of improper conduct by a physician.

As in court malpractice actions, the prosecution and defense call on medical authorities to testify as experts, and the panelists weigh their conflicting opinions in deciding whether the defendant adhered to or departed from the community standard of care.

Physicians can appeal disciplinary proceedings and recommendations to the state courts, and on due process issues, the courts may decide in favor of physician-defendants, occasionally vacating or modifying health department rulings and remanding cases for a rehearing. Seldom, however, do the courts intervene on findings of fact. Here they generally defer to decisions by the state boards, presuming that judgments by hearing panels and Administrative Review Boards reflect a superior knowledge of medical matters.

Physicians treating persistent Lyme disease with long-term antibiotics have been prosecuted by medical boards in a number of states. These prosecutions have led doctors to feel hesitant about handling chronic or recurrent cases, forcing patients in some instances to seek treatment beyond their home states.

Two recently-decided medical board prosecutions in Michigan and NY illustrate that such Lyme physicians can succeed in establishing that their practice is based on a therapeutic approach shared by a substantial number of competent, respectable physicians; i.e., that there are two standards of community care in Lyme.

In 1996 the state attorney general filed a complaint with the Michigan Board of Medicine concerning the approach to treatment for Lyme disease followed by Dr. Joseph Natole. The attorney general alleged that Natole's treatment, given to 37 patients, did not meet the standard of care. An Administrative Law Judge (ALJ) considered the complaint, concluded that physicians were divided into two schools of thought about the diagnosis and proper therapy for Lyme, and found that the facts did not support major negligence charges against Natole.

Reviewing the ALJ's findings, the Medical Board found Natole negligent in all cases, suspended his license for six months, and placed him on probation for two years. Natole appealed the Board's ruling in court, maintaining that the Board had summarily dismissed the ALJ's opinion that there were two acceptable standards of care for Lyme disease. The court determined that the Medical Board recognized the existence of the two standards of care, but saw evidence in Natole's practice of relatively minor departures in the performance of "basic medical procedures."[2]

Dr. Joseph Burrascano was prosecuted by NY's Office of Professional Medical Conduct (OPMC) in 2000. Involving nine

---

2 See Joseph Natole, Jr., MD, Petitioner v Michigan Board of Medicine, Circuit Court for the County of Saginaw, MI: case No. 96-15560-AA

Lyme patients, the charges included: gross incompetence and negligence, fraud, failure to maintain adequate medical records, and the ordering of Lyme tests and treatment unwarranted in these cases. An OPMC hearing panel held that the facts did not support the charges relating to Burrascano's treatment of Lyme. The panel, though, did recommend placing him on probation for six months on the basis of four minor findings of negligence.[3]

What the hearing panel in Burrascano said with respect to the two standards of care for Lyme and the OPMC's role in the debate over proper treatment for persistent infection is worth quoting at length. While this opinion is not binding on any other state medical board, it should constitute persuasive authority in "sister" board proceedings against Lyme physicians:

"The Hearing Committee recognizes the existence of the current debate within the medical community over issues concerning the management of patients with recurrent or long-term Lyme disease. This appears to be a highly polarized and politicized conflict, as was demonstrated to this Committee by expert testimony from both sides, each supported by numerous medical journal articles, and each emphatic that the opposing position was clearly incorrect...What clearly did emerge, however, was that Respondent's approach [Burrascano's approach]... is one that is shared by many other physicians. We recognize that the practice of medicine may not always be an exact science 'issued guidelines' are not regulatory, and patient care is frequently individualized. We are also acutely aware that it was not this Committee's role to resolve this medical debate."

Lyme patients have succeeded in convincing state governments to initiate or pass laws aimed at preventing prosecution of physicians merely because they follow one of the two community standards of care for Lyme. Conjecture has pointed to health insurance companies unwilling to reimburse for extended antibiotic therapy as prime instigators in prosecutions of Lyme specialists who give antibiotics long-term, and testimony at government

---

[3] NY Board of Professional Medical Conduct, Burrascano, BPMC #01-265.

hearings suggests that pressure by insurers may figure in state board proceedings against Lyme physicians. Other factors may play a role, too. According to US Senate language contained in a Congressional appropriations bill passed in 2002, some medical boards appear to have confused CDC Lyme surveillance criteria with diagnostic guidelines in viewing departures from community standards.

WORKERS' COMPENSATION

All states have laws that provide money to pay for medical expenses and lost income when workers become ill or injured because of employment. Some states exempt several categories of employees, and a few states mandate coverage only where an employer has more than a set minimum number of workers. Separate federal laws compensate government, maritime industry, and railroad employees.

While the amount of compensation and certain other details vary in these laws, the requirements are generally alike. The key, invariable provision is that, in order to collect, employees do not have to show that injuries on the job resulted from employer negligence.

To qualify for compensation, workers must prove that their illness or injury directly arose from or during employment. Illness attributable to employment conditions that pose greater risks than those normally found in daily life are also compensable.

Employees who qualify receive fixed weekly benefits based on their usual salary. The benefits vary from state to state but generally range from half to two-thirds of regular wages per week. Compensation is paid over the period employees can't work. Permanently disabled workers are eligible for compensation for reduction in earnings attributable to the permanent nature of the illness or injury.

Note, in general, that ill or injured workers wanting to obtain payment for medical expenses and loss of income must file a claim under workers' compensation with the employer as soon as possible. Payment for lost wages and medical expenses are made by the employer's insurance company.

Should an employer challenge a claim, a workers' compensation board in each state schedules a hearing, takes evidence, and determines whether and how much compensation is owed. Both workers and employers can appeal compensation board decisions.

People who work outdoors in regions known to be inhabited by ticks are at the greatest risk of exposure to Lyme disease. They comprise the majority of employees who file compensation claims for job-related Lyme. To cite a typical case: In August 1989 a man who had served for many years as an insulation foreman for a business owned by his family was supervising installation of pipes at a construction site in Suffolk County, Long Island, NY. Trees and shrubs surrounded the site, located in a region endemic for Ixodes ticks. On September 10th, the man was admitted to a hospital with complaints mimicking a heart attack. In reply to a questionnaire, he could not recall a tack bite. Testing in October, however, showed borderline evidence of possible Lyme infection. A test in March 1990 gave a positive finding for Lyme.

His compensation claim was contested by the insurance carrier, arguing that he was unable to pinpoint the date of injury and that he had notified the insurer after the filing period had expired. A NY State Workers' Compensation Board took the case, hearing evidence which included testimony by a medical expert on Lyme disease that the whole Long Island region had an exceptionally high density of Ixodes ticks.

In a Memorandum of Decision dated May 7, 1997, a Workers' Compensation Board judge ruled that the claimant's inability to pinpoint the date of the tick bite didn't preclude his claim, and that under the circumstances of the case the insurer was not prejudiced by the delayed filing. The judge also found that on the basis of the "credible evidence" of the medical expert, the claimant "was exposed to Lyme Disease as a natural incident of the claimant's employment as an outside worker in eastern Suffolk County. Consequently...Lyme Disease for this claimant was an occupational disease."[4]

As mentioned earlier here, certain federal laws cover workers' compensation claims for persons employed by the government, maritime industry, or railroads. Contested claims by such employees are adjudicated in the federal district courts. An

---

4 Arthur M. Lach v Island Insulation Contract Co.,NY, WCB# 2911 8147.

action brought under the Federal Employers' Liability Act (FELA), decided in 1993 by the US District Court, Southern District of NY, serves to exemplify these cases. This particular case involved four employees of the Long Island Railroad Co. (LIRR), all claiming they were disabled by Lyme disease contracted while working on an electrification project at various Suffolk County sites during 1987 and 1988.

The Court considered testimony by medical experts for the plaintiffs and the defendant, the LIRR, concluding that the defendant's expert was unable to contradict the testimony of the plaintiffs and their medical experts that they had, in fact, become infected by Lyme disease.

In its decision, the Court noted that FELA requires employers to provide workers with a reasonably safe workplace: this requirement includes the duty to maintain and inspect work areas. The Court found:

"The LIRR breached its duty to maintain and inspect work sites so that these areas might be reasonably safe for employees assigned to work there...The railroad knew or should have known by the summer of 1987 of the tick infestations and of the risk of infection...It was foreseeable that the employees would be bitten by ticks and thereafter infected with Lyme Disease."

Summing up its findings, the Court stated: "Plaintiffs established causation by a preponderance of the evidence, although not to a certainty. All four plaintiffs were assigned to work in tick infested areas...and within weeks or months...manifested symptoms of Lyme Disease. All were subsequently diagnosed as having Lyme Disease. The Lyme Disease contracted by all four plaintiffs was caused by their working in unsafe areas where they were doing their jobs, as they were required to do, in connection with their employment by defendant LIRR."[5]

---

[5] Grano v Long Island RR Co., 90 Civ. 2407(RJW); US Dist. Ct, Southern Dist., NY 818 F. Supp. 613; 1993 U.S. Dist.

Workers in densely urban areas remote from Lyme tick habitats occasionally become infected, filing claims for compensation. In 1996 a women serving as a technician for NYC's Emergency Medical Service (EMC) transported an elderly man to a city hospital by ambulance. His body was covered with lice and ticks, and so many "bugs" (her word) dropped off onto the woman's arms that she had to take a disinfectant shower at the hospital.

At home she continued to discover ticks, tweezing them out of her skin, and continued to wash with a special shampoo. Examination at a doctor's office two days later found only red marks and pin holes. No EM rash appeared, but after several days she experienced characteristic manifestations of Lyme infection.

Over time, she developed chronic recurrent fever, confusion, depression, dizziness, extreme fatigue, joint pain, and slurred speech (among other conditions). Altogether she had to be hospitalized more than 30 times. A physician diagnosed Lyme in 1997, conducted extensive, repeated medical tests, and referred the patient to other medical specialists. None proposed an alternative diagnosis. Nonetheless, the woman's employer contested her claim. The Worker's Compensation Board held hearings (through 2001), reviewed her history (which included no opportunities for exposure to Lyme elsewhere), heard expert witnesses, and decided the claim in her favor in 2002. In a memorandum on its decision, the Board noted that "Lyme disease has been established in numerous workers' compensation cases," citing five NY cases along with the essential specifics.[6]

---

[6] Memorandum of board panel decision in the case of Denise Chapman, WCB Case #0972 0507, NY.

DISABILITY CASES

CDC data indicate that children are most at risk for Lyme disease, so this portion of the law section of the *Lyme Disease Update* focuses on the protection against discrimination afforded students with Lyme by federal disability statutes.

Until the early 1970s, the due process and equal protection clauses of the Fourteenth Amendment to the US Constitution provided Americans with general safeguards against discrimination because of disability. Congress provided specific protections through passage of the Rehabilitation Act of 1973, the Americans with Disabilities Act of 1990 (ADA), and the Individuals with Disabilities Education Act of 1997 (IDEA).

In the 1973, 1990, and 1997 Acts, the definition of the term "disability" is basically the same: To qualify, an individual must be physically or mentally impaired to the point where the disability substantially limits at least one major activity of life. Individuals with a record of such impairment, and individuals who may be regarded as having such an impairment, can also qualify. Note that the last meaning of the term "disability" covers people whose major activities are not substantially limited by a physical or mental impairment, but their employers believe them to be substantially limited by such a disability.

Section 504 of the 1973 Act essentially prohibits an entity receiving federal financial assistance for its activities and programs from denying qualified disabled persons the right to participate in or benefit from these activities and programs. The section covers public and private recipients, stipulating that if any program or activity of an entity receives federal funds, all the entity's programs and activities are then required to comply with 504's provisions. Enforcement of Section 504 in educational institutions is mostly carried out by the federal Office for Civil Rights (OCR).

Titles II and III of the ADA go beyond prohibition of discrimination against qualified disabled individuals by entities with federally-funded activities and programs. Title II prohibits public entities from denying a person with a qualifying disability the right to benefit from or participate in activities, programs, or services these entities provide - if the exclusion or discrimination is based on the person's disability. Title III covers places of public accommodation, prohibiting entities from denying qualified disabled people equal and full use of the accommodations, advantages, facilities, privileges, and services that these entities provide. The OCR enforces Title II. The Department of Justice (DOJ) enforces Title III. There are some exemptions from compliance, depending on whether an entity is public or private, or receiving or nor receiving federal financial assistance.

IDEA was enacted by Congress in 1997 with four purposes in mind:[7]

1. To see that all American school-age children with disabilities have access to appropriate, free, public education fitting their unique needs and preparing them for independent living and employment. This includes designing special education programs and related services, and it involves assisting federal agencies, states, localities, and educational service in providing such an education.

2. To assist each state in implementing a statewide, comprehensive, and coordinated system of early intervention services for disabled pre-school children and their families.

3. To ensure that both educators and parents have the necessary specialized tools to improve educational results for disabled children.

4. To assess efforts to educate children with disabilities, thereby ensuring the effectiveness of these efforts.

The 1997 Act has to do mainly with specific procedures required to see that every disabled child receives a free appropriate public education (FAPE). Thus, it is especially important that boards of education and parents familiarize themselves with these

---

[7] IDEA, www.special-ed-law.com: the web site of Sussan & Greenwald, Attorneys at Law, East Brunswick, NJ.

requirements and fully appreciate the rights of disabled children under IDEA's provisions.

Essentially, IDEA obliges school districts to identify disabled and potentially disabled children, classify them, and refer them to a Child Study Team that will develop an Individualized Education Program (IEP), monitor the IEP, and revise it as needed. The 1997 Act sets forth all procedural rights, specifically enumerating how parents are involved.

CLAIMS FOR INSURANCE COVERAGE OF TREATMENT

Because of the number of health care insurers in the private and public sectors and the variableness of the coverage provided by their coverage plans, the best course in seeking reimbursement for medical services when an insurer refuses coverage or denies a claim for medically necessary treatment is to acquaint oneself with the provisions of the particular plan. If it appears that coverage should be provided according to the plan, then the next step is to find out whether the plan calls for compulsory arbitration in settling disputed claims. If not, suing the insurer in court for a coverage claim may be the only recourse.

Increasingly across the US, in insurance cases, the term "medical necessity" is being interpreted by the courts as the standard of community care for the illness involved. There are two legally accepted approaches to care in Lyme disease (see the discussion earlier in this section on medical malpractice), and in persistent or recurrent cases treated with long-term antibiotics, insurers have been quick to shield themselves behind the standard enabling them to reject or restrict a claim for reimbursement of treatment.

In Logan et al v. Empire Blue Cross & Blue Shield, a suit brought in the NY Supreme Court, six NY patients with chronic Lyme claimed that Empire had denied pre-authorization for antibiotic therapy. All the plaintiffs had bought their medical care privately. ERISA (Employee Retirement Income Security Act), a federal law that covers insurance plans offered by employers to employees, limiting extra-contractual and punitive damages, did not apply to four plaintiffs. It did apply, however, to two plaintiffs, and their claims were disqualified. (The area of insurance law involving ERISA is under considerable flux. To date, at least 10 states have passed laws curtailing the ERISA preemption. ERISA's impact on obligations applicable to insurers under state laws, though, is beyond the scope of discussion here.[8])

---

8 Johnson L & Stricker RB, Treatment of tick-borne diseases: a medicolegal assessment; paper awaiting publication.

Ira Maurer, an attorney in Westchester Co., NY, who has tried a variety of cases involving Lyme, filed a deposition transcript of a videotape as part of the public record in the Logan case around 2001. The person videotaped was Empire's chief medical officer, and in the tape the medical officer described how Empire had recently reviewed coverage costs, finding that a small number of cases accounted for a disproportionate percentage of payouts. These cases involved patients with catastrophic illnesses, Lyme disease among them. Empire then reworded its corporate medical guidelines on reimbursement for such conditions, making it more difficult for some patients to prevail in contesting a denial of a claim, even when some of these patients were clearly entitled to the medical care prescribed.

Note in connection with Logan that court cases decided against insurers seldom appear on the public record. As a condition for payment of a contested claim, the insurers tend to seek "gag" orders forcing all parties and all lawyers to remain silent perpetually about the terms of settlement and the payouts. The prime worry on the part of insurers is setting a binding public precedent.

Glossary

acrodermatitis chronica atrophicans (ACA): A skin condition affecting the extremities, characterized by lesions with abnormal redness of the skin (due to capillary congestion) and abnormal accumulation of serous fluid. The lesions tend to atrophy, giving the skin the appearance of wrinkled tissue paper.

antisera: Serums containing antibodies.

aseptic: Free from organisms, such as bacteria and viruses, that cause disease.

ataxia: An inability to coordinate voluntary muscular movements; symptomatic of some nervous disorders.

AV: abbreviation of atrioventricular (relating to an atrium and ventricle of the heart)

axonal: Adjectival form of axon, a long and single nerve-cell process that usually conducts impulses away from the cell body.

Babinski signs: A reflex movement where the great toe turns upward instead of downward when the sole of the foot is tickled; normal in infancy but a sign of damage to the central nervous system in later life.

Bannwarth's syndrome: A meningoradiculoneuritis that occurs in Lyme disease, the most common neurological manifestation of Lyme disease in Europe. It is characterized by a CSF lymphocyte pleocytosis, intense radicular pain (especially at night), and usually lacks typical signs of meningitis, e.g., headache, naseau.

B-lactam: Beta-lactam antibiotics are a large group of antibiotics having a lactam ring, such as penicillin and cephaloporin. Lactams are amides of amino carboxylic acids characterized by the grouping -CONH - in a ring.

bleb: A small blister-like structure.

BSK-II: One of a number of mediums or nutrient systems for artificially culturing (growing) cells or organisms, especially bacteria.

BUN: Blood, urea, nitrogen. It refers to the concentration of nitrogen in the form of urea in blood.

cerebellar ataxia: The cerebellum is a part of the brain situated between the brainstem and the back of the cerebrum. It is involved with coordinating muscles and maintaining bodily equilibrium. Ataxia is defective muscular coordination, especially voluntary, caused by cerebellar disease.

chorea: Any of a variety of nervous disorders marked by spasmodic movements of the limbs and facial muscles and loss of coordination; chorea may be infectious or organic in origin.

clonus: A series of alternating contractions and partial relaxations of a muscle; occurs in some nervous diseases in the form of convulsive spasms.

cranial neuritis: An inflammatory or degenerative lesion of a nerve in the cranium or skull; marked by sensory disturbances, pain, and impaired or lost reflexes.

CSF: Cerebrospinal fluid.

cytolysis: Dissolution or disintegration of live cells.

demyelination: Destruction or loss of myelin, the soft white material forming a protective sheath around some nerve fibers.

dermatome: Lateral wall of a somite, from which the dermis is produced. (A somite is one of the longitudinal series of segments into which the body of many animals is divided. The dermis is the sensitive vascular inner mesodermic layer of the skin.)

diaphoresis: artificially induced copious perspiration.

differential diagnosis: A process for distinguishing one disease or condition from others with similar manifestations.

diplegia: A paralysis of corresponding parts on both sides of the body (both legs, for example).

distal: Adjective meaning situated away from the point of attachment, or origin, or a central point.

electromyography: A means for graphically representing the phenomena of muscle contractions.

electrophoresis: The motion of charged particles, particularly colloidal ones, through a relatively stationary liquid or gel under the influence of an applied electric field, usually produced by immersed electrodes.

ELISA: Acronym for enzyme-linked immunosorbent assay.

encephalitis: Inflammation of the brain.

encephalomyelitis: A concurrent inflammation of the brain and spinal cord.

encephalopathy: A brain disease, especially one involving alterations of brain structure.

epineural vessels: Epineural used as an adjective means arising from the neural arch of a vertebra. A neural arch is the cartilaginous or bony arch enclosing the spinal cord on the dorsal side of a vertebra. Dorsal used as an adjective in anatomy means in, near, off, on, or toward the back.

ESR: Abbreviation for erythrocyte sedimentation rate. (Erythrocytes are red blood cells.)

eucaryotic: Adjectival form of eukaryote, an organism that consists of one or more cells containing evident nuclei and organelles (a specialized cellular part analogous to an organ).

extrapyramidal: Located outside of and especially involving descending nerve tracts other than the pyramidal tracts. (Corticospinal tract is another name for a pyramidal tract.)

febrile: Feverish.

flagellar: Adjectival form of flagellum, a long tapering process projecting singly or in groups from a cell, which is the primary organ of motion in many microorganisms.

fluorography: The photographic record of x-ray images produced by a fluoroscope; a process where a fluoroscopic image is photographed onto film using a lens camera.

Guillain-Barre: Usually called Guillain-Barre syndrome. A polyneuritis of unknown cause characterized by muscle weakness and paralysis.

hematuria: Presence of blood or blood cells in urine.

hemolysis: Lysis (i.e., break-down, decomposition, disintegration) of red blood cells, freeing hemoglobin.

hepatomegaly: Enlargement of the liver.

heterogeneity: A state consisting of or involving dissimilar elements or parts; a mixture of such parts.

hyperacusis: Abnormally acute hearing.

hypoglycorrhachia: Decreased amount of glucose in CSF, usually occurring in meningitis.

hyponatremia: Deficiency of sodium in the blood.

hyporeflexia: Underactivity of bodily reflexes.

IgA: Immunoglobulin A. A class of antibodies found in external bodily secretions (such as saliva, sweat, tears).

IgG: Immunoglobulin G. A class of antibodies including those most commonly circulating in the blood; active against bacteria, proteins foreign to the body, and viruses.

IgM: Immunoglobulin M. A class of antibodies of high molecular weight; includes those appearing early in the immune response; replaced later by IgG of lower molecular weight.

immunogenic: Producing or relating to an immune response.

intraerothrocytic: Occurring or situated within red blood cells.

intrathecal: Adjective meaning introduced into or occurring under the arachnoid membrane of the brain or spinal chord. The arachnoid is a thin membrane of the brain and spinal chord lying between the dura matter and pia matter.

kinetics: Study of the effects of forces on the motions of material bodies or with changes in a chemical or physical system; also, the rate of change in such a system; also, the mechanism for effecting such chemical or physical changes.

keratitis: Inflammation of the cornea of the eye; caused either by infectious or noninfectious agents; marked by blurring of vision, sensitiveness to light, burning, or smarting.

lability: A frequently or readily changing or fluctuating state.

leukocytosis: An increase in the number of leukocytes (white blood cells) circulating in the blood.

leukoencephalitis: Inflammation of the brain's white matter.

leukopenia: A condition in which the number of leukocytes circulating in the blood is unusually low.

L-form: A variant form of bacteria usually lacking a cell wall.

lymphocytic meningitis: Lymphocytes are colorless, weakly motile cells, originating from stem cells. Typical cellular elements of lymph, they include the cellular mediators of immunity, and constitute 20 to 30 percent of the leukocytes (white blood cells) in normal human blood.

lymphopenia: Reduction of the number of lymphocytes circulating in the blood.

lysis: A process of disintegration or dissolution (as in cells).

macules: Anatomical structures in the form of spots differentiated from surrounding tissues.

maculopapules: Small bodies projecting from the skin marked with spots.

meninges: Three membranes enveloping the brain and spinal chord.

meningitis: An inflammation of the meninges.

meningopolyneuritis: Meningo is a combining form of meninges. Polyneuritis is an inflammation of several peripheral nerves in the membranes covering the brain and spinal chord.

merozoites: A merozite is a small ameba-like sporozoan, usually reproducing by multiple segmentation, capable of starting a new asexual or sexual cycle of development; Sporozoans constitute a large class of parasites, which often generate in different hosts and include the pathogens for malaria and babesiosis.

mitogenic: Adjective referring to mitosis, the process of cellular division in which the nucleus forms two new nuclei, each having the same number of chromosomes as its "parent."

mononeuritis multiplex: A neuritis that affects several separate nerves.

morbidity: A disease manifestation or state; also the incidence of a disease (rate of sickness in a specified community or a particular illness).

morphea: Localized scleroderma, a progressive skin disease marked by the depositing of fibrous connective tissue in the skin and often in internal organs.

myelitis: Inflammation of the spinal cord or of the bone marrow.

myoclonus: A condition characterized by irregular involuntary contraction of a muscle.

myopericarditis: Inflammation of both the pericardium and myocardium. The former is the conical sac of serous membrane that encloses the heart and the roots of the great blood vessels, and the latter is the middle muscular layer of the heart wall.

mycoplasma: Genus of minute pleomorphic gram negative microorganisms, intermediate between viruses and bacteria, without cell walls, mostly parasitic, usually in humans.

neuropathy: An abnormal and usually degenerative state of the nervous system or nerves.

neurotropic: Adjective meaning with an affinity for or selectively localizing in nerve tissue.

nocturia: Night urination, particularly when excessive.

oligoclonal immunoglobins: Two to five bands of immunoglobulins. Each band is in a protein secreted by plasma cells They are found in spinal fluid and blood serum in some persons and are often indicative of diseases of the CNS.

paraparesis: Partial paralysis affecting the lower limbs.

paresis: Slight or partial paralysis.

parasitemia: Presence of parasites in the blood; used to indicate the presence of parasites without clinical symptoms.

paresthesia: A sensation of creeping, pricking, or tingling on the skin. It has no objective cause; usually associated with irritation or injury of a sensory nerve or nerve root.

pathogen: A specific cause of a disease; for example, a bacterium or a virus.

periarticular: Adjective meaning of, occurring in, related to, or being the tissues surrounding a joint.

periventricular: Adjective meaning situated or occurring around a ventricle, especially a ventricle of the brain.

petechiae: Plural of petechia, a minute reddish or purple spot containing blood that appears in mucous membranes or skin in some infectious diseases.

phagosomes: Membrane-bound vesicles that engulf particles taken into cells by phagocytosis, a process in which cells (often white) consume foreign matter and debris, which serves to defend against microorganisms and against debris and foreign particles that occlude mucous surfaces or tissues.

photophobia: Painful sensitivity to strong light; sometimes an intolerance to light.

plasmacytes: Plasma cells.

plasmid: Extrachromosomal ring of DNA replicating independently, found especially in bacteria.

pleocytosis: An abnormal increase in the number of cells in the cerebrospinal fluid.

pleomorphism: Noun form of pleomorphic, an adjective meaning able to assume different forms.

polyneuropathy: A nerve disease, especially one that is noninflammatory and degenerative.

pneumonitis: Disease marked by inflammation of the lungs.

proteinuria: Excess protein in the urine.

psychogenic: Originating in the mind or in emotional or mental conflict.

radicular: Adjective meaning of, related to, or involving a nerve root.

radiculitis: Inflammation of a nerve root.

radiculoneuropathy: An abnormal, usually degenerative disease of nerve roots.

reticuloendothelial: Being or related to the diffuse cell system that arises from the mesenchyme, and comprising all the phagosomes except for circulating white blood cells. The mesenchyme is part of the embryonic mesoderm out of which the circulatory and lymphatic systems, connective and skeletal tissues develop. The mesoderms is the middle of the three primary germ layers of an embryo.

Reiters Syndrome: A disease characterized by conjunctivitis, recurrent arthritis, and urethritis; usually initiated in individuals genetically predisposed to develop this condition.

sensorium: The portion of the brain that functions as the center of sensations; also, the sensory apparatus of the body as a whole.

serology: A science concerned with the properties and reactions of serums.

serum: The clear yellowish fluid remaining after whole blood is separated into its liquid and solid components.

SPECT: Single Photon Emission Computed Tomography.

spheroplast: A cell with a partial cell wall remaining after lysis of gram negative organisms.

spirochete: A slender, spirally-undulating bacterium belonging to the order Spirochaetales; included in this order are bacteria that cause (among other diseases) Lyme borreliosis, relapsing fever, and syphilis.

splenomegaly: Abnormal enlargement of the spleen.

sural nerve: Any of several nerves in the calf of the leg.

synovitis: Inflammation of a synovial membrane, usually with swelling and pain of the joint.

thalamus: Largest subdivision of the diencephalon, mainly consisting of the nuclei in an ovoid mass in each lateral wall of the third ventricle of the brain, serving to relay impulses, especially sensory ones, to and from the cerebral cortex. The diencephalon is the posterior subdivision of the forebrain.

thrombocytopenia: Persistent decrease in the number of blood platelets, often associated with hemorrhagic conditions.

T2-signal: A signal from the second thoracic nerve. T is an abbreviation of thoracic; used with a number from 1 to 12 to indicate a specific vertebra or segment of the spinal cord.

tetraparesis: Muscular weakness of all four extremities (legs and arms).

titer: The concentration of a substance in solution or the strength of a solution as determined by titration (the chemical process which determines the concentration or strength).

vasculitis: Inflammation of a blood or lymph vessel.

vegetative: Engaging in or relating to nutritive and growth functions, as contrasted with reproductive functions.

vestibular: Of or relating to the vestibule of the inner ear, the vestibular nerve, the vestibular apparatus, or the labyrinthine sense. A vestibule is any of various body cavities.

Based on:

Merriam-Webster's Medical Dictionary

Taber's Cyclopedic Medical Dictionary

Encyclopedia of Medical Imaging, Vol 1

American Heritage Dictionary of English Language, 4th ed., 2000

General Practice Notebook, A UK Medical Encyclopedia on the World Wide Web

An online encyclopedia, Http://encyclopedia.thefreedictionary.com

About the Author

Marcus A. Cohen

Since the mid-980s, Marcus Cohen has devoted himself to expansion of plausible medical options and empowerment of patients. He has scheduled and appeared on numerous radio and TV shows dealing with the politics of health care, including a Donahue Show on alternative treatment in 1992, for which he was chief consultant. In 1993, he testified on FDA regulation of dietary supplements and in 1993 and 1994, he testified before the New York State legislature on physician discipline and reimbursement for cancer screens and experimental treatment. In August, 1997, the National Institutes of Health (NIH) invited him to attend a 3-day conference convened to discuss a proposal by the National Cancer Institute and Office of Alternative Medicine for a practice outcomes monitoring and evaluation system. He again testified in NY on physician discipline in 2002.

Mr. Cohen's commitment to therapeutic breakthroughs, mainstream and alternative, widened in the fall of 1993, when he served as chief consultant for a 2-day seminar on new directions in cancer treatment, co-hosted by then Congresswoman Susan Molinari and former Congressman Guy Molinari. Conversations with scientists at prominent research institutions suggested that clinical practice may soon undergo a broad paradigm shift. The chief impetus for this shift comes from insights emerging from advances in molecular biology, human genomics, and nutrition research. Therapeutic protocols derived from these insights are aimed at modulating the early stages of disease–when treatment is often less invasive, more effective, and less costly.

Since Sept. 2001, Mr. Cohen has published eight articles in the *Townsend Letter for Doctors and Patients,* a national monthly. These articles detail how the state medical board in New York, established to discipline substandard doctors, has prosecuted physicians offering minority treatment approaches that benefit patients unresponsive to standard care. Through 2005, he will be publishing monthly columns under the byline Townsend's NY Observer. He is currently writing a book about the cancer research and treatment complex called *The Cancer Labyrinth*, covering both conventional and non-conventional therapy.

Mr. Cohen lives in New York City.

About the Editor

Patricia (Pat) V. Smith

Pat Smith, Monmouth University graduate, lives in New Jersey. She is the president of the national Lyme Disease Association (LDA), a 501 (c)(3)non-profit group dedicated to Lyme disease education, prevention, research funding, and patient support. She is Vice President for Political Affairs of ILADS, International Lyme and Associated Diseases Society, a professional medical and research organization. Ms. Smith, former chair of the (NJ) Governor's Lyme Disease Advisory Council, is a former 12-year member of the Wall Township Board of Education where she earned state board member-certified status and was past president.

She has been an active advocate for Lyme and education issues for many years, and has testified/lobbied/educated at all governmental levels.

Under her leadership, the LDA has provided nationwide grants for LD research, a number of which have resulted in published peer-reviewed research articles. Ms. Smith was responsible for the development of LDA's *LymeR Primer, The ABC's of Lyme Disease* pamphlets, and *Tickmarks* (bookmarks). She has worked on the development and passage of State and federal bills for Lyme research, prevention, and physician education. Ms. Smith has appeared on a number of television programs in many states including Fox TV's *Good Day, New York* and has been quoted in publications including *Newsweek, Washington Post, USA Today,* and *People* magazine. Her article on avoiding Lyme disease, entitled "Lyme Disease: A Tick Away," was published in 2000 in *Great Outdoors* magazine. She is a member of the ILADS working committee that authored and published

"Evidenced-based Guidelines for the Management of Lyme Disease" in the peer-reviewed journal, *Expert Review of Anti-Infective Therapy*, 2004.

Ms. Smith has led the effort for the LDA, collaborating with Time for Lyme, its affiliate, in partnering with Columbia University to open the first of its kind endowed research center for chronic Lyme disease at Columbia. Additionally, she has worked with *New York Times* best-selling author Amy Tan to create LymeAid 4 Kids, a fund through LDA to help children whose families have no insurance coverage for Lyme disease to be evaluated for Lyme disease.